Healing

Insights for Christian Elders

Ron McKenzie

Kingwatch Books

Kingwatch Books
Christchurch
New Zealand
www.kingwatch.co.nz

Contents

Warning

This book is full of principles, but on their own, principles achieve nothing. Principles cannot heal the sick. The presence and power of the Holy Spirit heal the sick, so he is what we need. The only value of the principles outlined in this book is that they may help Christian elders who are walking in the Spirit to understand what he is doing and know how to cooperate with him as he advances the Kingdom of God and brings glory to Jesus.

Second Warning

This book is for the future, so the Holy Spirit may not yet have prepared you to receive the message that it contains. If the approach disturbs you, please lay the book aside and wait until the time is right.

Cover Image

The hydrangea bloom appears like a large oval flowerhead, but is actually made up of a dozen of small flowers. Each flower looks the same, but each one must be in the right place. If as single flower is missing, the overall shape will be distorted. This is a lovely picture of the body of Christ. For the church to get victory over sickness, every part of the body will need to be in the right place and blossoming in the gift that God has given them. Victory over sickness will come as the body of Christ comes to fullness.

1
Two Streams

Introduction

Over the last few years, I have been wrestling with the issue of Christian Healing. I have watched some really strong Christians being beaten about by serious sickness. Although they have kept a good attitude, their sickness does not seem to have glorified God. Rather, the effectiveness of their ministry has been severely limited. Their experience has really bugged me, because it does not fit with the scriptural promises about healing.

The Bible seems quite clear. Jesus' gift of salvation includes both forgiveness and healing of sickness. For example, Psalm 103:2-4 says:

> Praise the LORD, O my soul,
> and forget not all his benefits-
> who forgives all your sins
> and heals all your diseases,
> who redeems your life from the pit
> and crowns you with love and compassion.

Forgiveness and healing are part of the same package. Jesus confirmed this by making the healing of the sick an important part of his ministry.

Our lack of victory over sickness raises a serious question. If healing is not a core part of our salvation, why did Jesus spend so much time healing the sick? If salvation does not include healing, his emphasis on healing was just giving a false hope. One suggestion is that God gave Jesus healing power to authenticate his ministry. This might be true, but surely the Holy Spirit needs to have his ministry authenticated as well?

Victory over sickness and eternal life both depend on the work of the cross, so I have to ask this question. If we cannot obtain victory over sickness through the cross, how can we be certain of eternal life based on the work of the cross? Actually, I am certain about eternal life, so I can only conclude that the problem is with our understanding of healing and salvation. Our gospel of healing seems to be deficient. Is there something missing?

While wrestling with these questions, I have searched the scriptures. During this search, I found some important keys that I hope will empower God's people to greater victory over sickness. A complete list of the keys is on page 115.

Warning to Readers
I am aware that many Christians have prayed against sickness for a long time without gaining victory. Reading this book may not provide much comfort to you. Some of you may even be left feeling condemned. The reason is that I am not writing for sick people, but for church leaders and elders. Most of the blockages to healing are problems with the church, so solving them will require changes in the way that elders fulfil their calling. In order to get Christian elders thinking, I have discussed some tough issues in a very direct way that could seem insensitive to those struggling with sickness. I apologise if this offends some, but I want a breakthrough that will prevent others from suffering.

Most of the problems lie with the church, so individuals battling with sickness will be powerless to do much about them, except challenge their elders to some serious thinking. The major issue is the general lack of faith throughout the church and no individual can deal with that on their own. Unless you are surrounded by a church or group of friends that is willing to grapple with some tough issues, the keys outlined here may not be of much help to you.

Key 1: Healing Flows in Two Streams

I have always been fascinated by the healing miracles in the gospels and the Acts of the Apostles. The way the Holy Spirit worked with the apostles was really exciting. However, I was always puzzled by James 5. I could not see how it fitted with the rest of the teaching about healing in the New Testament. James' message seemed so tame in comparison to Acts and the Gospels. A couple of years ago, I discovered that there are two streams of teaching about healing in the Bible, and suddenly everything fell into place. If we split the teaching of the scriptures into these two streams, God's strategy for healing makes more sense.

A. Healing and Evangelism

The gift of healing is primarily for unbelievers as a demonstration of the love of God. The Gospels and Acts describe how the gift of healing works in evangelism. Jesus brought good news to apostate Israel, so his ministry often demonstrated this type of healing.

B. Healing and Believers

The second healing theme explains how God's people can walk in health. Healing is part of salvation, so it should be a normal part of every believer's life. James is a key passage in this second stream.

The healing of unbelievers and believers has a different basis. One is based on mercy and the other on covenant.

> Healing of the unbeliever is based on the mercy of God.
> Healing of the believer is based on the covenant.

Unbelievers are in the kingdom of darkness, so it is normal for them to be sick. They can only be healed, if God breaks in with power and mercy that they do not deserve. They need the gospel to get out of the kingdom of darkness.

God will sometimes extend mercy to an unbeliever to prove his existence and mercy and love. He does not do this just for the benefit of the person healed, but for all those who see the miracle. He releases his power to shake people up and make them ready to receive the gospel.

On the other hand, Christians get sick, when something is wrong. They have not received everything that they are entitled too. Christians are living in Christ, so they should be experiencing all the benefits of the cross. They are entitled to the healing earned when strips of flesh were ripped off Jesus' back. This makes it odd for Christians to be sick.

The solution is not physical power, but removing the obstacle that is preventing the Christian from receiving what Jesus has earned for them. If they cannot sort that out on their own, they will need help from someone else with greater faith or wisdom. This is why the scriptures tell sick Christians to go to their elders (James 5). A variety of things can make a Christian sick: lack of faith, sin, demons, ignorance of the gospel or spiritual strongholds. Their elders should seek God for the reason. When they understand the cause, they can deal with it and allow the sick person to receive the health that Jesus has bought for them.

The cause of sickness is different for unbelievers and believers, so the solution must be different. Their healing is appropriated in different ways.

.

2
Healing for Non-Christians

The most important truth that Christians need to understand is that the gift of healing is for unbelievers. It is mainly for evangelism and not for Christians. Jesus' ministry was mostly evangelistic. He came to save the lost, so when healing the sick, he was often ministering to people without faith to receive the benefits of the cross. Therefore, much of his healing ministry belongs in the first stream. Similarly, many of the healings in the Acts of the Apostles were received by unbelievers.

The healing of an unbeliever in an evangelistic situation is based on the mercy of God. The person healed is not entitled to the benefits of the cross, because they have not yet surrendered to Jesus. The Father lets them have the benefits of the cross in advance because he is merciful.

Jesus had a unique method of evangelism. He would preach the gospel and then heal the sick and cast out demons to confirm his message. Here are two examples.

> Jesus went throughout Galilee, teaching in their synagogues, preaching the good news of the kingdom, and healing every disease and sickness among the people (Matt 4:23).

He went down with them and stood on a level place. A large crowd of his disciples was there and a great number of people from all over Judea, from Jerusalem, and from the coast of Tyre and Sidon, who had come to hear him and to be healed of their diseases. Those troubled by evil spirits were cured, and the people all tried to touch him, because power was coming from him and healing them all. Looking at his disciples, he said:

> Blessed are you who are poor,
> for yours is the kingdom of God (Luke 6:17-20).

Jesus' method was to go to a town and pray for someone who was sick. When a crowd gathered to see what had happened, he would preach his message. The healing confirmed Jesus' message by demonstrating the power and compassion of God. When they saw the sick being healed, his listeners could not deny the reality of God, or his mercy in Jesus. Jesus gave the same commission to his disciples.

When Jesus had called the Twelve together, he gave them power and authority to drive out all demons and to cure diseases, and he sent them out to preach the kingdom of God and to heal the sick (Luke 9:1-2).

As you go, preach this message: "The kingdom of heaven is near." Heal the sick, raise the dead, cleanse those who have leprosy, drive out demons. Freely you have received, freely give (Matt 10:7-8).

The healings demonstrated the mercy of God. The pattern is:

- receiving authority;
- preaching the gospel;
- healing the sick.

All Christians have the same authority to preach the gospel and heal the sick. Jesus promised that,

These signs will accompany those who believe: In my name they will drive out demons... they will place their hands on sick people, and they will get well. Then the disciples went out and preached everywhere, and the Lord worked with them and confirmed his word by the signs that accompanied it (Mark 16:17-20).

Jesus promised that God would confirm the preaching of the gospel with signs and wonders. Peter and John experienced this when they went to the temple and God healed a lame man. An amazed crowd gathered, so Peter preached to them. Several thousand came to faith in Jesus, because God had given authority to Peter's words before he started to speak. The same was true for Paul and Barnabas.

> Paul and Barnabas spent considerable time there, speaking boldly for the Lord, who confirmed the message of his grace by enabling them to do miraculous signs and wonders (Acts 14:3).

The Holy Spirit loves to prove bold preaching of the gospel with gifts of healing and deliverance. This changes the nature of evangelism.

Normal New Testament evangelism is based round the healing of the sick. This is confirmed in Acts 8:5-6:

> Philip went down to a city in Samaria and proclaimed the Christ there. When the crowds heard Philip and saw the miraculous signs he did, they all paid close attention to what he said.

The passage says that the Samaritans were amazed at the miracles, but only records that Philip preached the gospel. Luke just assumed that proclaiming the gospel included healing and miracles.

Modern Evangelism

Modern evangelistic campaigns are very different. The outreach meeting is often held in a church building, so a powerful publicity campaign is needed to get people to attend. The evangelistic method is preaching a sermon, giving an altar call and getting decisions. This method has had some success, but it is not the New Testament way.

New Testament evangelism is healing the sick/casting out demons, preaching to the crowd that gathers, baptising those who believe. This method was very successful for the early church, so we are unwise to adopt a different method.

Sickness is the key vulnerability of the modern world. Our affluent lifestyle has given people almost everything they need, but modern medicine has not been able to conquer sickness. A gospel confirmed by healing of the sick will be well received. Jesus said,

> I am going to send you what my Father has promised; but stay in the city until you have been clothed with power from on high (Luke 24:49).

If we do not have the power that we need for New Testament style evangelism, the answer is simple: we should wait until the power from on high comes to us (see also Acts 1:4-5). I suspect that God would prefer that we do some serious waiting, so that we can do evangelism his way, rather than rushing into doing evangelism our way.

Healing should be a normal part of evangelism. The good news is that God is merciful, but a cynical world does not believe our claims. Healing demonstrates God's mercy and proves that Jesus is the Saviour. The best visual aid for the gospel is someone who is visibly sick being healed (the other is baptism).

Strategy for Evangelism

Healing Evangelism should use the following strategy.

1. Evangelists must understand their **authority over sickness**. Jesus destroyed the power of sickness and sin and gave his followers authority over them. There are no limits to his authority and power. He healed:

   - all diseases (Matt 4:23),
   - all people who came to him (Matt 12:15), in
   - all places (Luke 9:6).

   Jesus' authority has not changed (Heb 13:8) and he has given the same authority to us.

2. When going to share the gospel, evangelists should be led by the Spirit. They should go to a place where God has

prepared people and wants to touch them. This will usually be a public place where a crowd is likely to gather. Jesus was always in the right place at the right time (John 5:19). He exercised his ministry in public, but always where the Holy Spirit was moving.

> One day as he was teaching… And the **power** of the Lord was **present** for him to heal the sick (Luke 5:17).

> And the people all tried to touch him, because **power** was **coming from him** and healing them all (Luke 6:19).

Evangelists should learn to recognise the power of the Lord to heal. They should be led to the place where the Holy Spirit wants to gather a crowd to hear the gospel.

3. Once in the right place, the evangelists should then *identify the person* that the Father wants to heal. When he went to the Pool of Bethesda, Jesus chose the paralysed man out of the great number of sick people waiting by the pool, because he was the one that the Father wanted to touch (John 5:3).

The Holy Spirit will often point out the person to be healed, but sometimes the person will come to the evangelist. The lame man at the gate of the temple came to Peter and John asking for money, but the Holy Spirit wanted him healed (Acts 3:3). When Paul was at Lystra, he saw a lame man whom the Holy Spirit had given faith to be healed (Acts 14:8-9). The evangelist should listen carefully to the Holy Spirit to identify the person God wants to heal.

4. The evangelists should lay hands on the person and *command* them to be healed in the name of Jesus. If the Holy Spirit has indicted that he wants the person to be healed, he will do what he said he would do and make the person whole.

5. When a person is dramatically healed in a public place, a crowd will usually gather. One of the evangelistic team should take the opportunity to **preach to the crowd**. They will explain that the healing is a demonstration of the grace of God and the power of the gospel.

6. The process will often involve **drama and noise**; the louder the better, because a bigger crowd will come. When Peter and John raised the lame man, a great tumult filled the temple area. The temple authorities were stirred up, but thousands came to the Lord.

7. The evangelists should be prepared to **pray for everyone** who comes seeking healing. When they see what the Holy Spirit can do, many will come wanting a touch from God. They will be looking for God's mercy, so he will not disappoint them. In the evening after Jesus had healed Peter's mother-in-law, the whole town gathered at the door and Jesus healed many who had various diseases (Mark 1:30-34). The same thing happened when Paul prayed for a sick man on the island of Malta.

   > His father was sick in bed, suffering from fever and dysentery. Paul went in to see him and, after prayer, placed his hands on him and healed him. When this had happened, the rest of the sick on the island **came and were cured** (Acts 28:8-9).

8. An evangelist should always follow the **leading of the Holy Spirit** (Acts 10:38, Luke 6:19). He is the one who heals, so we must let him operate in the way he chooses. For the man by the pool of Bethesda, healing came before repentance, whereas the paralytic lowered through the roof repented before he was healed. The order can be:
   - belief/deliverance
   - deliverance/belief
   - healing/deliverance
   - deliverance/healing.

The Holy Spirit will know the order required. We should be careful not to be locked into one way of operating. The human tendency is to find something that works and then flog it to death. "Pray and Slay" is the current fashion. In contrast, Jesus always ministered in ways that were different and unique. He healed blind people in five different ways.

- touching the eyes   Matt 9:29
- spitting on the eyes   Mark 8:23
- declaring they could see   Mark 10:52
- commanding the eyes to open   Luke 18:42
- rubbing clay and saliva on the eyes   John 9:6-7

He touched one leper, but told the ten to go and show themselves to the priests. If evangelists listen to the Spirit, a similar variety of methods will be present in their ministry.

9. Jesus sent his disciples out in pairs. When preaching the gospel and healing the sick, Christians should work in a group of two or three, or more.

   - There is power in agreement. Jesus promised that when two or three people work together, he would be with them (Matt 18:19-20, Acts 3:4-5).
   - Working in a group strengthens the body by releasing the gifts of the Spirit and faith.

Failures

Praying for the sick is a very risky business, due to the fear that nothing might happen. We are not perfect like Jesus, so we will have some failures. Some of the people that we pray for will not be healed. We must be prepared to be humble and accountable. If the person is not healed, we must deal with it.

We should never blame the sick person. We must be careful not to blame sick people for lack of faith, because it does not make sense to expect unbelievers to have faith. We must not blame God, as that would insult the gospel and deny his mercy. It is better to say that our faith is too small than to let the person blame God or themselves.

We should use the experience of failure to learn. It is okay to go to Jesus and ask (privately) why someone was not healed.

> Why couldn't we… (Matt 17:19).

Jesus will answer and teach us how to do better next time.

Reasons Why People are not Healed

There are a number of reasons why unbelievers may not be healed in the context of evangelism. (They are not explanations for Christians being sick).

1. Failure to Command

Jesus always commanded sickness to leave. He would address the person and command the sickness. Here are some examples of his words:

Leper	Be clean
Little girl	Get up
Paralytic	Take up your bed and walk
Deaf	Be opened.

He sometimes made a declaration: "You are healed" (Mark 5:34,39). He sometimes told the sick person to do something and they would be healed. He sometimes declared that the person was already healed.

Jesus never asked God to heal a sick person. Likewise, the apostles never prayed for the sick, but always commanded sickness to leave. We must understand the authority we have in Christ. We must not ask Jesus to heal people, because he has given us authority to do it (Matt 10:1).

2. Not Enough Faith

Lack of faith is probably the main reason for unbelievers not being healed. Faith is essential for healing (Acts 3:16), but it can have different sources.

- The sick person may have faith to be healed.
    Paul looked directly at him, saw that he had faith to be healed (Acts 14:9).
  This level of faith will be rare amongst unbelievers, as it is very hard for a person who is chronically ill to have faith.

- Friends of the sick person may have faith. This was the case with the paralytic man lowered through the roof.
    Jesus saw their faith… (Luke 5:20).
- The evangelists will usually have to be the ones with faith (Acts 3:1-7). They will have faith, because they understand their authority.

Faith is inescapable. Nothing will happen without it. The more miracles that evangelists see, the more their faith will rise (John 2:23).

3. More Prayer Needed

Mark 8:22-26 records that Jesus had to pray for a blind man twice. After the first prayer, he could see, but not properly. Jesus had to pray a second time to heal his mind, so he could understand what he was seeing. If Jesus had to pray twice, we should not be ashamed to pray more than once. Some serious sickness may need continuous prayer (2 Kings 4:32-35).

4. Lack of Discernment

Mark 7:33-35 and Matthew 9:32-33 describe the healing of two different people who could not speak. They had the same symptoms, but the diagnosis and the solution were different. One had a physical impediment and could be healed by command, whereas the other had a demon that needed to be cast out. The symptoms were the same, so discernment was needed to know what to do. If a sick person is not healed, a demon may need to be cast out. Ideally, this should be discerned before seeking a healing.

5. Sin

Unconfessed sin in the evangelistic team may render their prayer ineffective. Before praying, the group should make sure they are at peace with the Lord and with each other. The group must be in unity. Pride is particularly dangerous when praying for the sick. Once we have seen a couple of people healed, we can start to think we are experts. That sort of pride usually comes before a fall. We can only heal the sick under the anointing of the Spirit (Luke 5:17), so grieving him will make us powerless.

The sin of the sick person is not relevant, because they are dead in the stuff. The purpose of healing is to dig them out of it. Jesus did not worry about the sin of the man by the pool, until after he was healed. He then told him to "Go and sin no more" (John 5:14). Once saved, sin can be an issue.

6. Compassion

Healing must never become a technique to win people for Jesus.

> When Jesus... saw a large crowd, he had compassion on them and healed their sick (Matt 14:14).

The gift of healing must flow out of compassion. Healing without compassion does not reflect the love of Jesus.

7. Wrong Place

We all want to see the Holy Spirit healing the sick, but we forget where it happens. Here are two passages that provide a key to successful evangelism

> And wherever he went—into villages, towns or countryside—they placed the sick in the marketplaces. They begged him to let them touch even the edge of his cloak, and all who touched him were healed (Mark 6:56).

> As a result, people brought the sick into the streets and laid
> them on beds and mats so that at least Peter's shadow
> might fall on some of them as he passed by (Acts 5:15).

Large numbers of people were healed in the streets and the market place. This is where the Holy Spirit prefers to work. I suspect that he sometimes gets bored with our meetings and longs to get out into public places and heal the sick. If we want to see him doing this, we should follow him.

Local Localities

The Holy Spirit works locally, not globally. He is not interested in large audiences or getting on television. He prefers to work in a particular locality with local people. When Peter's mother-in-law was healed, the entire neighbourhood came with their sick. They realised something special was going on, because they knew Peter and his mother-in-law. Some that had seen her with the fever saw her again healed. They did not need further proof.

As soon as healing goes onto the public stage, questions are asked. Was the person really healed? Were they pretending to be sick to get close to the great preacher? Were they as sick as they claimed? Did the sickness come back next week? Has the healing been authenticated by their doctor? God does not need this junk.

The Holy Spirit prefers to work locally. The people living close by will know the person who is healed. They can quickly work out for themselves if the healing is real. When Jesus healed the man who was blind from birth, "his neighbours and those who had formerly seen him begging" could see that his vision was restored (Jn 9:8).

One reason that we do not see as many healings as we would like is that we look in the wrong places. We expect people to be healed on the stage at the front of a church. The Holy Spirit prefers to work locally. We should be taking him out to the sick people in our neighbourhoods.

Key 2: The Gift of Healing is for the World

Going into the world with the gift of healing is very important. Over the last decades, God has been restoring the gift of healing to the church. This is great, but we have tended to keep it in the church and only prayed for Christians. This is a serious mistake.

Praying for Christians is a good way to learn about healing, but we need to go on to praying for the people of the world. If we do not, we will lose the gift. The Holy Spirit loves the world and is always moving out towards it to draw people to the Father (John 7:37-38). If we do not go with him, he will go on without us.

Jesus blessed us so we could bless others. If we are just seeking our own healing, we are missing the point. We should be seeking healing for unbelievers who are in pain. When sending out the disciples to heal the sick, Jesus said,

> Go the lost sheep… (Matt 10:6).

We should go to the lost sheep of the world.

Obey Jesus

Jesus instructed the church how to do evangelism in Mark 16:15-20. He said we should go into the world (not stay in the church) and preach the gospel. We should expect God to confirm our gospel message by healing the sick and other signs. This method has always been successful. It worked for the twelve and the seventy-two when Jesus sent them out. When the latter returned, Jesus saw Satan falling from heaven (Luke 10:18). Jesus' method worked for Peter and John when 5000 people came to the Lord after a lame man was healed (Act 3,4). The same method worked for Paul in Malta, even though he was a prisoner (Acts 28:1-10).

Strangely, the church has ignored this method of evangelism throughout most of history. We dream up other methods of evangelism, like inviting an evangelist to the church and getting people to bring their friends (they rarely do). We put on a concert or user-friendly worship to bring people to the church, but we stubbornly refuse to use the method of evangelism that Jesus specifically commanded. We should not be surprised that we do not have revival.

Christian elders should be training evangelists with the anointing to heal the sick and sending them out of their churches into the world to demonstrate the love of God by healing the sick and preaching the gospel. This would bring revival.

3
Christians and Healing

Getting the Paradigm Right

The modern church has its wires crossed. Most healing prayer for Christians is done by the pastor at the front of the church, or by an evangelist at a healing meeting. The process is quick and dramatic, but it usually fails because the wrong paradigm is being applied in the wrong place.

Slam bam, "Be healed in Jesus name" works for unbelievers, because all they need to be healed is a burst of God's power. It does not work for Christians, because the underlying cause of the sickness is not resolved. Finding out why the person is not able to receive what Jesus has freely given may take time, words of knowledge, talking about issues, or confession of sins. This is unlikely to happen at the front of a meeting.

If their problem is lack of faith, a Christian may get inspired at a healing meeting and have a rise of faith to the point where they are healed. That is great, if it happens. However, lack of faith is only one possible cause of sickness. Many other issues that rob people of the healing that Jesus has earned for them cannot be dealt with on the stage at the front of a church. Peace and quiet are needed to hear the Lord and sort out the problem.

The healing-meeting method belongs in the world for people who have not received the gospel. The big-man, healing-meeting model does not work for sick Christians, because it is using the wrong method in the wrong place. The fact that most churches are full of sick people is proof. Many have gone forward for healing many times, but they are still sick. The large numbers of Christians who are sick after fifty years of healing meetings are evidence that the model is faulty. We have ignored God's clear teaching and it is costing us dearly.

Elders are the Key
James 5 is very clear. Sick Christians should go to the elders. It does not say they should go to the doctor. It does not say to go to a healing meeting when an anointed evangelist is at a church in town. It does not say they should go to the church meeting next Sunday. It says that they should go to the elders.

Elders have avoided this issue for a long time. Christians have let them off the hook by ignoring the command and going to doctors and healing meetings. However, if we deliberately ignore God's command, we should not be surprised that numerous Christians are sick.

Paul did not see a church full of sick Christians as something normal. He saw it as a sign that something was wrong.

> That is *why* many among you are weak and sick, and a number of you have fallen asleep (1 Cor 11:30).

The word "why" refers to a cause or reason. Paul saw excessive sickness as a sign that something was seriously wrong. One reason that sickness is so pervasive in the modern church is our unbiblical model for the healing ministry.

Healing for Christians is totally different from the healing of unbelievers. This is the second stream of healing in the Bible. The healing of Christians is based on the covenant.

Key 3: Understand the fullness of our Covenant

Christians need a revelation of the fullness of the covenant that God has established with us. We must understand that healing is part of our covenant inheritance.

God does not get sick. Humans were created in the image of God, so there was no sickness before the fall. The Tree of Life protected Adam and Eve from sickness. After they sinned, they were cut off from the Tree of Life. Their sin placed them under a curse and brought sickness into the world (Gen 3:24).

Sickness is part of the curse of sin. Just as the Holy Spirit is a deposit, guaranteeing our inheritance (Eph 1:13-14), sickness is a deposit, guaranteeing death. Sickness is the firstfruits of death and a constant reminder of our frailty.

Old Covenant

Under the Old Covenant, sickness, plagues and epidemics were part of the curse of sin (Deut 28:21-22,27-28). Full health was promised to those who obeyed God.

> Worship the LORD your God, and his blessing will be on your food and water. I will take away sickness from among you, and none will miscarry or be barren in your land. I will give you a full life span (Ex 23:25-26).

This passage is not hard to interpret. God promised that those who serve him will be free from sickness and will live a full life span.

The experience of Moses confirmed this promise. He was one hundred and twenty years old when he went to be with God, but his eyes were not dim and his body was not weak (Deut 34:7). Caleb was as strong at eighty years of age, as he had been when he was a young man (Joshua 14:7-8,10-12).

> The righteous will flourish like a palm tree,
> they will grow like a cedar of Lebanon;
> planted in the house of the LORD,
> they will flourish in the courts of our God
> (Psalm 92:12-13).

The promise of the Old Covenant is clear and good. Unfortunately, the promised blessings are conditional on obedience. Most people found it impossible to achieve the level of righteousness needed to be free of sickness (Heb 11:13,39-40). They never entered into the promised blessing, because they failed to obey God.

New Covenant

The New Covenant is a better covenant, containing better promises (Heb 8:6). The promises of the Old Covenant were not received due to disobedience and lack of righteousness. Jesus' death on the cross changed this situation by providing perfect righteousness for all who believe in him. He paid the penalty for sin and disobedience, earning the benefits of the covenant for those who have faith in him (Heb 9:15). We no longer have to live a perfect life to receive freedom from sickness. Freedom from sickness is part of our inheritance in Jesus.

Jesus died on the cross to deal with the effects of sin. As sickness is an effect of sin, it was dealt with on the cross (Gal 3:13). Healing is part of the salvation package that Jesus established for his people. The Greek word for save (σοζω sozo) also means "heal". The salvation established on the cross dealt with both sin and sickness. Jesus restored everything that was affected by sin, including sickness.

Matt 27:26-30 records that Jesus was flogged, spat on and struck with a rod. This suffering was not needed to pay the penalty of sin, as his death was all that the law required for sin. The additional beatings were for our healing. This was to fulfil what was spoken through the prophet Isaiah:

> He took up our infirmities and carried our diseases (Matt 8:17).

1 Peter 2:24 quotes the same verse. Our health was bought by Jesus' flogging, in the same way that the cross dealt with sin.

Health is part of our inheritance in Jesus, but although millions of people have claimed forgiveness of sin through the cross, very few have received the healing that was bought by his flogging. Since he bore our sickness for us, we should not still be bearing it. If we deny that his salvation includes healing, we are wasting the pain and agony of his beating.

Disease is Dead

Jesus carried our sicknesses and carried our diseases when he died on the cross. They died with him when he died (Rom 6:5,8). They did not rise again when he rose from the dead, so they are still dead, and must stay dead.

When Jesus rose from the dead, we rose with him (Rom 6:4), but our sicknesses and diseases did not. We are alive, but they are dead.

We can declare that our bodies were raised and restored with Jesus in the spiritual realms, so they must be healed and whole in us on earth. When we command a sick person to "be healed", we are declaring them to **be** on earth, as they **are** in Jesus in heaven.

Real Pain

The spiritual powers of evil use the curses of the old covenant to demand the right to inflict sickness and disease on those who forget God. Jesus accepted a physical beating to nullify their right to inflict pain on us (1 Pet 2:23). He could not just take our sickness and diseases away. He had to experience real physical pain and weakness to free us from sickness and disease.

Everyone wanted to have a go at him, so he was beaten several times.

- The Jewish guards beat him (Luke 22:63).
- The members of the Sanhedrin struck him with their fists or slapped him (Matt 26:67).
- Pilate had Jesus flogged (John 19:1-2)
- Roman soldiers struck his head with a wooden staff again and again (Matt 27:30).

After these beatings, Jesus' entire body would be in agony.

The spiritual powers of evil cannot claim that his pain was not real, because he experienced pain equivalent to our sicknesses and diseases. It was sufficient to provide us with health and healing.

New Christians
Most Christians should be healed when they are saved. If the evangelist is praying for the sick, most who receive the gospel will be healed. This should be normal practice, because the full gospel includes healing.

> As you go, preach this message: 'The kingdom of heaven is near.' Heal the sick, raise the dead, cleanse those who have leprosy, drive out demons. Freely you have received, freely give (Matt 10:7-8).

If these words are fulfilled, those who receive the gospel will be healed. The gospel package includes forgiveness, deliverance, release from demons and the gift of the Spirit. Healing is part of the package available to those who believe.

We need a radical rethink on this issue. A new Christian is a new creation (2 Cor 5:17). The old has gone and the new has come. If a proud man with chronic bronchitis and a spirit of anger were born again, we would expect him to become humble. We would want him to be free of the spirit of anger. Why should we expect his chronic bronchitis to remain? These things are all part of his old life, so they should go.

In practice, it should be easier to deal with sickness than sin. Learning to be humble might take a while. The man might be tempted to get angry again, but he would be unlikely to want his chronic bronchitis back. Jesus said,

> Which is easier: to say, 'Your sins are forgiven,' or to say, 'Get up and walk'? (Luke 5:23).

Sickness is easier to deal with than sin. Sickness took a word, whereas sin required his death on a cross.

Walking in Health

Jesus is our model. He is the standard against which we measure our lives. There is no evidence that Jesus was ever sick. He never failed to turn up at a meeting because he had a cold. He never took time off his ministry, because he was down with the flu. The idea of Jesus being sick does not make sense. If Jesus was full of health, his followers should be too.

Jesus' victory over sickness means that health is normal for God's people. Full health is part of the salvation that he has given to us. Despite these facts, sickness is pervasive in the church. This suggests that there is something wrong with our understanding of salvation. In this book, I attempt to crack through this conundrum. I believe that the problem is with us and not with God. The first step to a solution is to understand the causes of sickness among Christians.

Satan is the Cause of Sickness

The clear message of the scriptures is that Satan is the cause of sickness. Sickness is an attack by the spiritual powers of evil. Peter attributed all sickness to the devil.

> God anointed Jesus of Nazareth with the Holy Spirit and power, and… he went around doing good and healing all who were under the power of the devil, because God was with him (Acts 10:38).

Most observers just see sick people, but Peter saw people under the power of the devil. Jesus made an interesting comment when he healed a crippled woman on the Sabbath.

> Then should not this woman, a daughter of Abraham, whom Satan has kept bound for eighteen long years, be set free on the Sabbath day from what bound her (Luke 13:16).

The people saw a woman who could not straighten up. Jesus saw a woman bound by Satan. We must see what Jesus sees.

Satan is the cause of sickness. He comes to steal, destroy and kill (John 10:10). Our health is part of what he is stealing and destroying. Job's friends saw severe boils and sores. The Holy Spirit says that this was an attack of the devil (Job 2:7).

Sickness is the most common evil attack that we experience. It is Satan's second most powerful weapon. If we are sick, he has a foothold in our lives. He can use it, when he chooses, to control us.

Christians blame Satan for too much sin. Most sin is really caused by our flesh. On the other hand, we do not blame enough sickness on Satan. He is responsible for most sickness among Christians. He gets away with this, because he has deceived us into believing that he is not the cause. He is happy being wrongly blamed for our sin, if it stops us from seeing that he is the cause of our sickness.

In Jesus, we are able to repel all the attacks of the enemy.

> God anointed Jesus of Nazareth with the Holy Spirit and power, and... he went around doing good and healing all who were under the power of the devil, because God was with him (Acts 10:38).

The key word is "all". All sickness is caused by the power of the devil. The Good News is that Jesus was able to heal all those afflicted by him, because he was anointed with the Holy Spirit and power.

The Physical is Irrelevant

We need discernment to deal with sickness. Too many Christians only see the physical side of sickness. They see it as caused by contact with an infection. This is not a Christian view, but is rooted in the modern philosophy of naturalism or materialism, which assumes that only the physical is real. Materialism explains all events in the universe through biological, social, genetic, environmental or physical interactions. All events are determined by cause and effect, with no spiritual or external influence.

The Bible teaches a different worldview. In God's economy, nothing happens by chance. Random events do not strike Christians. Everything in our lives has a spiritual side to it. Everything that happens on earth is an interaction between the workings of God and the machinations of the enemy.

> For our struggle is not against flesh and blood, but against the rulers, against the authorities, against the powers of this dark world and against the spiritual forces of evil in the heavenly realms (Eph 6:12).

Although events may appear to have a physical cause, the real cause is spiritual. For example, Eli the high priest was blind and could not see (1 Sam 4:15). A physical examination would have shown that Eli had cataracts. However, the scriptures teach that he was blind because he refused to do anything about the sins of his sons. He "turned a blind eye" to sin (1 Sam 2:29).

An inspection of Job's body would have discovered a staphylococcus causing his boils, but the Bible explains that they were actually caused by an attack of Satan (Job 2:7). King Asa sought help from the King of Damascus. He died from an infection in his feet, but the reason was that "even in his illness, he did not seek help from the Lord" (2 Chron 16:13).

Jesus healed numerous sick people. In each case, it would have been possible to diagnose the infection causing the disease, but from God's point of view, they were "under the power of the devil" (Acts 10:38). Jesus healed a woman who had been bent over for so long that she could not straighten up. A physical examination would have diagnosed osteoporosis in her spine, but Jesus said, "Satan has kept her bound for eighteen years" (Luke 13:16). Christians must learn to look beyond the medical facts and into the spiritual dimensions to understand the real cause of sickness.

Minimum Effort Evil

Despite the advance of medical knowledge, cancer still strikes fear. Cancer is a favourite method of attack for the spiritual powers of evil (John 10:10).

They tend to attack the best people. They love cancer, because it enables them to kill and destroy good people who are making a difference in his Kingdom.

Cancer is a minimum effort evil for the powers of evil. All they need to do is to corrupt a few cells somewhere in a human body, so that they divide and grow rapidly. For a long time, the tumour will be too small to be noticed, but it is a ticking time bomb. When the time is right, the disrupted cells become a large growth that makes the body sick. If left alone, the afflicted person will die.

The spiritual powers of evil have the skill to produce cancer cells, because they were around at the creation. They helped God create the plants and the animals, so they understood the structure of cells, better than we do.

After the fall, they had plenty of practice corrupting cells and species, during the millennium of evil. Causing a couple of cells to divide and grow rapidly is child's play for them.

The spiritual powers of evil like to work with reproductive organs, because they love to destroy life. Their favourite place is the bowel, because they are comfortable working amongst the excrement of life.

Starting a cancer takes minimum effort, because once a couple of evil spirits have corrupted the cells and set them growing and dividing, they do not need to do anything more. They just wait, and send a spirit of fear to cripple the person further when the time bomb is discovered.

Stolen Strategy

The spiritual powers of evil never do anything creative. They are just doing what they learned to do at the creation, but with a destructive twist.

The idea of rapidly growing and dividing cells was God's plan for the body of Christ. When a group of believers has grown, he wants the best leaders sent out as apostles to start a new group. This process can be repeated numerous times. This strategy was successful for the early church, but for most of history, God's people have rejected his plan.

The devil has stolen the divide and grow method and used it to attack the physical bodies of Christians. The sick person becomes anaemic as the growth in their body accumulates and amasses. In contrast, most churches have rejected the divide and grow method and chosen instead to amass and accumulate. They build bigger buildings and try to draw more people in, but this makes them anaemic.

Permission to Attack

The devil is the cause of all sickness, but his powers are limited. In principle, he cannot attack a Christian. He has free reign over those who are not Christians, because they are part of the kingdom of darkness. He can inflict sickness on them whenever he chooses, but Christians are different. We have been rescued from his dominion and brought into the kingdom of light (Col 1:13). We are covered by the blood of Jesus, so he is not allowed to touch us.

Satan can generally only inflict sickness on a Christian, if he gets permission. Before he could touch Job with boils, he had to get permission from God (Job 2:6). If God had refused, Satan could not have harmed Job. Likewise, Satan cannot strike a Christian without getting permission from someone with authority in their lives. God is not going to give that permission, so he has to get it from us. Christian elders must be careful not to give the devil authority to attack people who have submitted to them.

Key 4: Evil affects us Three Ways

Satan is the cause of all sickness. He inflicts sickness in three ways.

1. **Sin** gives Satan permission to attack us with sickness. When we sin, we lose God's protection and leave our bodies vulnerable to Satan's junk.
2. **Deception** is the other way that Satan gets permission to hit us with sickness. He puts confusing words or thoughts into our minds. If we accept his deceptions, he gains some control.
3. **Direct Attack.** Satan is a cheat and will sometimes attack without permission, especially when a person is moving forward for God.

The method for dealing with sickness depends on how we have been attacked.

1. **Repentance** deals with sin.
2. **Revelation** dispels the deceptions that allow control.
3. **Resistance** repels a direct attack.

The cure must fit the cause. The Holy Spirit will reveal the cause, if we seek him. If a Christian cannot discern it, the elders of the church should be able to help. Once we understand the cause, defeating sickness is easier.

Spiritual Armour

Paul advises Christians to put on the armour of God so that they can stand against the devil's schemes (Eph 6). The spiritual armour can be viewed as protection against the three ways that sickness attacks us: sin, deception and direct attack. Two pieces of the armour are particularly useful for dealing with sin. Two others protect us against deception and control. The other two weapons are really effective against direct attacks of sickness.

The Holy Spirit can teach Christians how to defend each other with these weapons.

SPIRITUAL ARMOUR		
Sin	**Gospel of Peace** Meditating on the cross and the gospel is the best antidote to sin.	**Breastplate of Righteousness** Righteousness in Christ protects us from sin and condemnation.
Deception and Control	**Helmet of Salvation** Jesus' salvation protects our minds and prevents deception.	**Belt of Truth** Truth about God is the best protection against the deception and control.
Direct Attack	**Sword of the Spirit** We can use the word of God as a sword to resist direct attacks of sickness.	**Shield of Faith** Faith resists the attacks of the enemy. The promises of God are received by faith.

4

Sickness through Sin

Christians must face the fact that we sometimes get sick because our sin gives evil access to our lives. This truth is unpalatable, but inescapable. Sin gives sickness the right to enter into our lives.

We must be careful about this truth. Some sickness is the result of sin, but some is not. The blind man healed by Jesus is the exception that proves this rule.

> As he went along, he saw a man blind from birth. His disciples asked him, "Rabbi, who sinned, this man or his parents, that he was born blind?" "Neither this man nor his parents sinned," said Jesus (John 9:1-3).

This sickness was not caused by sin. Jesus could discern the difference. We must not assume that all sickness is caused by sin, but we must be aware that some sickness is caused by sin. Here is the truth.

- All sickness is caused by Satan.
- Only some sickness is the consequence of sin.

Types of Sin
I am a sinner, so the cause of my sickness will often be sin. This can happen in various ways. Christians should be aware of them all.

1) Personal Sin

Some sickness is the consequence of personal sin. Jesus spoke very directly to the man who had been paralysed when he found him in the temple again.

> See, you are well again. Stop sinning or something worse
> may happen to you (John 5:14).

If he continued in sin, he would experience more sickness.

Numbers 12:1-2 recorded that Miriam became leprous, when she was critical of Moses. David reports that he became sick after he sinned (Psalm 38:5-11). Asthma is sometimes caused by fear, and arthritis is sometimes caused by bitterness (see also Luke 1:20; 62-66, Prov 17:22; 15:30; 14:30). Job said,

> If I have raised my hand against the fatherless,
> knowing that I had influence in court,
> then let my arm fall from the shoulder,
> let it be broken off at the joint (Job 31:21-22).

He is suggesting that a painful shoulder can be caused by failure to assist the poor.

2) Diet and Hygiene

Sometimes the sin is not caring for our bodies. Lack of sleep and stress can make us sick. Prayer is not the solution to this sickness. We must do something about the stress to be healed.

The Bible has clear guidance on hygienic latrines and washing (Deut 23:11-14); quarantining infections, mildews and dead bodies (Num 5:1-4, 19; Lev 17). Ignoring this teaching is a sin that can cause sickness.

Sometimes the lack of care will be poor nutrition or bad diet. The scriptures provide good advice on diet (Lev 11, 17, Deut 14). God's people were warned against eating fat, long before heart disease became a concern (Lev 7:22). Leviticus warns that we should not eat blood (Lev 19:26). This advice is often ignored, because we don't like Leviticus.

Christians should not expect God to heal them, if their sickness is caused by inadequate diet or hygiene. Timothy had frequent sickness because he was drinking bad water and fasting excessively.

> Stop drinking only water, and use a little wine because of
> your stomach and your frequent illnesses (1 Tim 5:23).

Timothy was sinning by not caring for his body, the temple of the Holy Spirit. Paul suggested a change of diet rather than offering prayer to resolve this problem.

3) Lack of Rest

A day of rest is a creation principle, so lack of rest can be a cause of sickness. God created our minds and bodies with a need for a day of rest each week to recharge. He gave Israel the sabbath to ensure that they got the rest they needed. Jesus is now our rest, so keeping a sabbath is not necessary for holiness, but a day of rest each week is still necessary for good health.

Individuals are free to decide which day of the week will be their rest day. The day chosen can vary from week to week, if their employment requires. Rest is not the same as worship. For some Christians, Sunday is such a busy day, that they need a different day for rest.

The modern lifestyle is to work eight days a week and take a holiday once a year. Those who live that way will often get sick. The remedy for this sickness is a day of rest each week to reduce stress.

4) Family Sin

The cause of sickness may be a sin in the family. Children can be affected by the sin of their parents. Children who do not honour their parents can shorten their lives (Eph 6:3). Sometimes the sin that caused the sickness will have been committed by an ancestor, who has placed his family under a curse (Lev 20:20; Prov 26:2).

5) Church Sin

Sin in a church may be the cause of sickness. The church of Thyratira tolerated the spirit of Jezebel (Rev 2:20-23). This sin caused many in the church to be sick and depressed. The sin of church leaders can affect the church as a whole. The church in Corinth had meetings that manifested disunity in the body. Things that seem quite trivial to us resulted in serious sickness and some people had died.

> That is why many among you are weak and sick, and a number of you have fallen asleep (1 Cor 11:30).

6) City or Nation

The sin of a political leader can affect an entire nation. All Israel suffered a terrible plague, because David counted his fighting men in disobedience to God (2 Sam 24:15). The sin of one person in a position of authority can affect a nation (Gen 20:3,7,9,17).

Sometimes, the people of a city or nation may join together to sin (Exodus 32:35). If a city or nation has a common sin, this can result in a common sickness among its people. However, there is no common curse of sickness (Psalm 91:5-13). Christians do not have to share in the curse on their city or nation. In Exodus 9:5-6; 12:29-30, the Israelites were kept safe when the people of Egypt were cursed for sinning against God. He can keep his people safe in a sinful city or nation.

7) Corporate Stronghold

A corporate stronghold gets control of a city when the religious and political leaders all participate in a sin such as pride, intimidation or manipulation to enhance their leadership. This corporate sin allows the evil spiritual power behind it to gain control of the city.

If Christian leaders have given the evil spirit permission to be there, it may claim that they have surrendered their authority to it on behalf of Jesus. Christians in the city may be sick, because this stronghold is able to block prayers for healing. It may refuse to surrender to the name of Jesus, because it claims authority given "in the name of Jesus".

A corporate stronghold is put in place by civic and religious leaders unwittingly submitting to a powerful evil spirit, so it has to be broken by the current corporate leaders repenting. If they renounce the stronghold that is controlling their city, it will lose its power. They would also have to commit to forgoing the sin that has enhanced their power.

Key 5: Repentance Heals Sin

If a sickness is the result of sin, the first step is to determine who sinned. This is really important. We should not assume that the person who is sick is the one who sinned. The sin may have been committed by an ancestor, elder or political leader. Once we identify the sin and the sinner, we know what to do.

If the sin is personal, the solution is simple: repentance. If the sin has been persistent, the sick Christian may need to confess the sin to friends or to elders to get free. Discipling may also be helpful for getting victory over the sickness.

> Therefore, strengthen your feeble arms and weak knees.
> Make level paths for your feet, so that the lame may not be
> disabled, but rather healed (Heb 12:12-13).

If sickness is the consequence of the sin of a city or nation, the Christian will need to stand apart from that sin. They must be careful that they are not participating in the community's sin, but are standing with those who are resisting it. For example, if their city is resisting the Holy Spirit, the Christian should make sure that they are always walking in the Spirit. They should pray for the city and nation.

If sin in the church is the problem, the person should pray for a prophetic voice to expose the sickness. If the leaders refuse to change, the sick person may need to look for a safer church.

If the cause of the sickness is a family curse, it should be broken. In some lives, several different types of sin will be all mixed up together. Disentangling them and dealing with them in the right order will be a challenge.

Laying on of hands for healing is pointless if the sickness is the consequence of sin. Many in the church are going forward for prayer again and again, but are not being healed. One reason might be unrepented sin. Prayer for sickness is pointless, if sin is the problem.

Besetting Sin

Sometimes, a sickness will be the result of besetting sin. Many of us have particular weak points in our character that we battle with for much of our Christian life. (I suspect that Paul's "thorn in the flesh" was a besetting sin and not weak eyesight as is often suggested.)

An example of a besetting sin causing sickness can be seen in the life of Jacob. The weakness in his character was an urge to manipulate people whenever he got into trouble, rather than trusting in God. He even wrestled with God, rather than trusting him. God touched his hip and gave him a limp, to remind him of his weakness (Gen 32:31). Jacob could not be healed of his limp, until he got victory over the besetting sin that caused it.

If our sickness is caused by a besetting sin, we may not be healed until we get victory over it. This may take many years. Strong spiritual support from Christian friends and elders may speed up the process.

Reminder

Some sickness is caused by sin; but most is not. Suggesting that sickness is the consequence of sin can be a dangerous weapon. It can do terrible harm, if it is not used with wisdom and compassion. Blaming sickness on sin, when it is not the cause, dumps a load of guilt and condemnation on the victim. We should never tell a sick person that their sickness was caused by sin, without a clear leading of the Holy Spirit. Even when the Spirit leads in this way, we must challenge the person with gentleness and compassion.

5

Deception and Control

Sin sometimes gives Satan access to our lives, but most sickness is the result of spiritual deception. Our minds are a battleground. Deception is a very effective weapon against us, because once entrenched, it gets control. If the enemy can get us to believe lies about our health, he has control over us. If we agree with his suggestions, we have given him permission to implement them in our lives.

Evil Schemes
Paul warns us to be careful about the enemy's schemes.

> Finally, be strong in the Lord and in his mighty power.
> Put on the full armour of God so that you can take your
> stand against the devil's schemes (Eph 6:10-11).

Most Christians assume that we need the armour of God to protect us from the power of the enemy. We should get rid of this idea. Paul does not warn about the devil's physical power. As far as Paul is concerned, his powers are feeble, because he was completely destroyed by the cross.

> The reason the Son of God appeared was to destroy the
> devil's work (1 John 3:8).

We do not need spiritual armour to protect us from his power, because he is powerless. We need the spiritual armour to protect us from thoughts and suggestions that would give him control and allow him to harm us. We should stop worrying about his physical power, and learn to deal with his schemes.

If we are living in obedience to Jesus, Satan can only get permission to attack us through scheming. He must convince us to give him permission to attack us. He gains control by influencing us to agree with his deceptions. This is why we must be aware of his attacks.

> Take up the shield of faith, with which you can extinguish
> all the flaming arrows of the evil one (Eph 6:16).

The suggestions and deceptions of the enemy are the flaming arrows described by Paul. In biblical times, soldiers would attach some tar to an arrow and set it alight before it was released from the bow. These darts were fairly harmless, but became dangerous if they were not quickly extinguished. A dart could not penetrate a building, but if it were not removed, the entire building could be engulfed in flames. If they hit a person, their clothes might catch fire. Fiery darts must be extinguished quickly to prevent serious damage.

Key 6: Understand his Cunning Schemes

Satan uses a variety of schemes. He will rarely try to persuade Christians to enjoy sinning, because that would be a waste of time. His schemes are more subtle. When tempting Jesus, he suggested some ways he could fulfil his ministry. If Jesus had accepted these suggestions, he would have been defeated. Here are some of the schemes that Satan uses to rob us of our health.

1. An attack of sickness often begins with the acceptance of a false thought.

> God sends sickness.
>
> Sickness is normal.

By accepting these false thoughts, we allow Satan to make us sick. Once our thinking is shaped by his ideas, sickness has a foothold in our lives.

Some of these thoughts come directly from the enemy. Others come from the people we meet. Many are the product of our distorted imaginations (this should become less frequent as we grow into the mind of Christ). Where these thoughts come from does not really matter. They must be dealt with quickly, before they take hold.

2. Negative thoughts can build up layer by layer over many years to become a stronghold. It starts with a single thought, then another is added, then more and more. When the enemy has shaped my entire way of thinking about sickness, he has a stronghold in my life. It may have started with the thought that "God does not like me" when a parent makes a negative comment. That may build into "God does not care about me", after rejection by someone close. The next building block may be "God will not heal my sickness". The final thought might be, "God wants me to be sick".

The first deception opens the door a chink that leaves the Christian vulnerable to another deception. The second one pushes it further open. If we allow these thoughts to multiply over many years, they can grow into a stronghold of sickness.

3. Anxiety and worry increase the power of deception. Advertisers know that thoughts attached to an emotion become more powerful. This was confirmed by Peter.

> Cast all your anxiety on him because he cares for you. Be self-controlled and alert. Your enemy the devil prowls around like a roaring lion looking for someone to devour. Resist him, standing firm in the faith (1 Pet 5:7-9).

Anxiety can lead to our being devoured by the devil. When he suggests that something evil might happen, we

49

can start to ponder it. If we brood over it, we can become anxious. Once we become anxious, we have effectively agreed with the deception. If we do not deal with anxiety, we are giving the devil permission to have a go. Job made an interesting comment about his situation.

> What I feared has come upon me; what I dreaded has happened to me (Job 3:25).

Maybe Satan was able to afflict Job with boils, because he had feared this happening. Getting anxious about something gives it permission to strike.

Peter advises that self-control and faith are the remedy to anxiety. We have the power to accept or reject the thoughts that come into our minds. We can reject a bad thought from the enemy by countering it with a thought that expresses faith. Positive declarations destroy doubt.

4. Satan can use people from the kingdom of darkness to attack us. These attacks will usually be verbal. He hopes that malicious gossip or insults will cause us to harbour hateful thoughts. Christians will often be attacked physically. Paul was often beaten by enemies of the gospel. When attacked by the world, we must keep our hearts pure by rejecting all negative thoughts.

Twelve Controlling Deceptions

The enemy uses various thoughts and suggestions to get authority in our lives. He often does not use that permission immediately, but stores it up for a rainy day.

Strongholds come in many forms. Our grumbling shows where we are most vulnerable. The following deceptions can become a stronghold (2 Cor 10:4).

1. Satan rules

Satan's most successful deception has been to persuade Christians that he was not defeated by the cross. Many now believe that Satan is in control of life on earth and will rule until Jesus returns. This evil scheme has gained him a lot of power to mess up the lives of Christians.

2. Sickness is normal

Many Christians have accepted the idea that sickness is normal. We believe salvation is for all, but we believe that healing is only for some. We just accept colds in winter, and we accept infirmity in old age. This belief is not true. There were no permanently sick Christians in the New Testament.

Sickness is normal for those who have rejected the gospel, because they are still under the dominion of darkness, but it is not normal for Christians. Sickness weakens the body of Christ, so it should never be acceptable to us.

The belief that sickness is normal for Christians is the most serious "flaming arrow" that the enemy can put in our minds. Once we accept this idea, he has permission to make us sick.

3. God causes sickness

The idea that God causes sickness is one of Satan's cleverest lies, but it is still a lie. God is good, so he cannot cause sickness. There is no sickness in heaven, so it cannot come from there. The appearance of someone dying of cancer is enough to prove that it is not from God. It is obviously the work of someone evil.

One of the names of God is Yahweh Rapha (Exodus 15:26). This name means "God Heals". God is called "Healer" because healing is at the core of his being. God the Healer cannot be the cause of sickness. The suggestion that he causes sickness is an insult to his character and name.

Sickness and disease were brought into the world by the evil one. He created viruses and bacterial diseases. We should never allow him to blame his handiwork on God.

Jesus only did what he saw the Father doing. He never saw his Father making people sick, so he did not make people sick either. God is the Healer. Blaming God for sickness is a terrible blasphemy. We should never say,

> God sent me this sickness.

Persuading Christians to believe that God caused their sickness has been another very successful scheme. If God is responsible for the sickness, then resistance is pointless. Unfortunately, many Christians now believe that their sickness was sent by God.

4. Sickness is not in the atonement

Christians frequently ask if healing is in the atonement. This is odd. The answer to the question is not "Yes". The correct answer is that everything is in the atonement. Jesus' death and resurrection dealt with every effect of human sin.

5. Sickness is good

This is a related idea, but sickness is not good. The Greek words used for sickness in the New Testament are negative.

ασθενεια	asthenia	weak
κακωσ	kakos	evil
μαλακια	malakia	soft
αρρωστοσ	arrostos	feeble.

If I say that God has made me sick, I am really saying that God has made me feeble. That is nonsense, because he does not want his people to be weak. The most that can be ever said is that God brings good out of sickness, but that does not mean much, because he can work any evil for good.

Paul's visit to Galatia was the result of sickness (Galatians 4:13-14). He described it as weakness of the flesh. He was embarrassed at being sick and he expected the Galatians to despise him. However, he did not say that the sickness was God's will, although God used it to accomplish his purposes.

6. God is sovereign

This is a true statement, but the enemy twists it to mean that God does not always heal. Christians will sometimes explain why they have not been healed by saying, "God is sovereign". No one ever says they were not healed, because "Jesus is sovereign". This does not fit with our picture of Jesus. We do not say it out loud, but deep down, we think that God is meaner than Jesus.

The truth is that Jesus never refused to heal anyone who came. I cannot imagine him saying,

> God is sovereign, so I cannot be sure if you will be healed.

Jesus never said to anyone,

> It is not God's will for you to be healed.

When a leper asked to be healed, Jesus said, "I am willing" (Mark 1:40-42). This settles the argument. Many Christians believe that Jesus defeated sickness on the cross, but they are unsure if God will do it for them. The record of the leper is there to teach us a principle: God is willing to heal. Therefore, we should never say,

> It is not God's will for me to be healed.

We can say,

> I don't have enough faith to resist this sickness.
>
> I cannot deal with this sickness on my own.
>
> My pastor does not have enough faith.
>
> I still have sin that I need to deal with.
>
> My church does not have victory over sickness.

7. Sickness is suffering

A common scheme of the devil is that God gives us sickness to make us holy. This is not true (sickness usually brings out the worst in us). God does allow his people to suffer, but they should suffer for doing right or for the name of Jesus, not through sickness (1 Peter 4:12-17). In 2 Corinthians 11:23-27, Paul listed all the ways he had suffered for Jesus, but he never counted sickness as part of his suffering for the gospel. Suffering in the face of evil gives glory to God, whereas sickness does not.

Jesus never refused to heal someone because God had made them sick to improve their character. James 5:13-14 distinguishes clearly between suffering and sickness and gives different responses. If anyone is in trouble, he should pray, but if he is sick, he should call the elders. Trouble and sickness have different causes, so they require different responses. Biblical suffering does not include sickness.

8. Sickness is a friend

Many Christians welcome sickness as a friend. Most of us have used sickness as an excuse to avoid doing something we do not want to do, like work or meeting someone we do not like. When we do this, we are giving sickness authority in our lives. Sickness is a curse, so we should never use it or welcome it. It is the sign of the kingdom of darkness intruding into our lives, so we should hate it with passion.

> The Son of Man did not come to destroy men's lives, but to save them (Luke 9:56).

Sickness destroys lives, so it is opposed to what Jesus is doing. He came to save and heal lives.

9. Loose words

One of the enemy's evil schemes is to send sickness and see if we will give it permission to stay. Some people just accept it with casual words. We should be careful what we say about sickness, because we receive what we speak.

No one living in Zion will say, "I am ill" (Isaiah 33:24).

We should not say,

I have the flu.

This is submitting to sickness and giving it control in our lives. We would be claiming something from the devil for ourselves. It would be more correct to say,

I am being attacked by the flu.

We should not say,

I am getting a cold,

This is prophesying something we should hate. We can say,

I am being attacked by a cold, but I do not want it.

10. Pleading

Many Christians have been misled into thinking that they must plead earnestly with God for their healing. Of course, nothing happens. The reason is that God has already done everything that he can do for salvation (healing). There is nothing more that he can do to help, except increase our faith and knowledge of his love.

Christians should not be begging God to heal them. Pleading only makes sense, if we can change his mind. We often pray as if he is stingy, but might heal us if we plead fervently. This is nonsense. God is good. He wants us whole. He is not holding back his healing, waiting to see if we are desperate.

Some are pleading with Jesus, because they think he is kinder than God. We do not need to plead with Jesus for our healing, because he bought it when he was whipped and beaten. We were healed by his stripes. Pleading with him implies that what he did at the cross was not enough for us. Begging with a person who died on a cross to do something more is absurd.

A related deception is that God will give in if many people pray, especially if some are really important Christians. This is nonsense. God responds to faith. He is not impressed by big numbers or big ministries.

We can ask God to give us a revelation of his goodness and love. We can ask God to stir up his elders. We can ask God to increase their faith, but there is no point in asking God for what he has already done. That sounds like ingratitude. There is no example in the New Testament of anyone praying in this way.

> Dear God, please heal my sick brother.

The reason is simple. From God's perspective, the sick brother was healed when Jesus died on the cross. God has already done what has to be done. Jesus' work is finished. Everything that he can do has already been done. There is nothing more to ask for. The church should not be asking for healing, but it should be appropriating the health that Jesus has bought for us.

11. Perseverance changes God's mind

A related deception is the belief that perseverance will change God's mind. This odd idea is based on a false interpretation of the parable of the unjust judge recorded in Luke 18:1-7. Most Christians assume that the unjust judge represents God and that if we persist in prayer, he will eventually give in and let us have what we want. This interpretation is a terrible insult to God's character. The unjust judge actually represents the devil. He does not respect justice or care about people, but he is a lazy adversary. He does not want to surrender to God's will, but he is worn down by persistence and gives up, because he has no stamina.

The idea that God does not want to heal us, but can be pestered into changing his mind, is an insult to his name.

12. Sickness causes death

Most Christians assume that they will live until they get a sickness that cannot be cured. Death comes when fatal sickness strikes. This view is incorrect. There is a time for everyone to die, but the death of a Christian should occur when their work on earth is complete, not when sickness gets the better of them. Moses is a good example. He died when he had led the people to the Promised Land and his work was complete. Christians should be like Moses and die when their service to God is finished.

Isaiah prophesied a time when everyone would live a full lifespan.

> Never again will there be in it
> an infant who lives but a few days,
> or an old man who does not live out his years;
> he who dies at a hundred
> will be thought a mere youth;
> he who fails to reach a hundred
> will be considered accursed (Isaiah 65:20-21).

The prophecy mentions people dying, so it is not describing life in heaven. It is referring to a time on earth when a hundred years will be the normal lifespan and anyone not reaching it will be considered accursed. For Isaiah, this promise was still in the future, but Jesus has made it possible for us. (Some Christians will say that this passage is for the Millennium. Unfortunately, the millennium doctrine is another deception that robs Christians of their inheritance.)

Now that Jesus has dealt with sickness, we should be claiming this promise now. There is nothing more that he can do in the future, so we should expect this passage to be fulfilled in our lives. Some people will die young, but only because their work on earth is finished and God wants them to be with him.

Christians do not live until fatal sickness strikes. They should live until their work on earth is complete. Our lives should not end until we have finished all that God has given us to do. Some people in Corinth, who ought to be living, had died needlessly (1 Cor 11:30). That was a waste.

On the other hand, we should also be careful about holding people back when their lives are complete. By praying for healing, we can stop people from dying. This prayer is not appropriate if their work on earth is finished. In some situations, we may need to give God permission to take home someone that we love. This may be important if Satan is trying to stop them from dying (Jude 9).

Key 7: Revelation defeats Deception

The devil often uses deception and control to inflict God's people with sickness. Because he was defeated by Jesus on the cross, the solution is relatively simple. God's revelation is stronger than the enemy's lies. We must resist his lies with declarations of the truth. Paul advised Christians to take control of their thoughts.

> The weapons we fight with are not the weapons of the world. On the contrary, they have divine power to demolish strongholds. We demolish arguments and every pretension that sets itself up against the knowledge of God, and we take captive every thought to make it obedient to Christ (2 Cor 10:4-5).

Negative thoughts about sickness are "pretensions" opposed to God. If we agree with these pretensions, we give sickness a stronghold in our lives. The solution is to destroy them with a revelation of the true knowledge of God.

Resist Dangerous Thoughts

We must resist all thoughts that allow sickness to get a hold in our lives. The permissions that allow sickness to strike were often given many years before the sickness actually came. We must learn to resist every thought that gives Satan permission to inflict sickness on us. Here are some examples of the types of thought that we should resist.

I catch everything that is going around.

Someone at work has a cold, so I am sure to get it.

My mother and grandmother both died of breast cancer, so I will probably die the same way.

I have a weak chest. A cold always goes to my chest.

I get a headache, if I do not have enough sleep.

I feel a cold coming on.

My child gets lots of ear infections.

These thoughts are half true, but agreement with them can give sickness permission to harass us, so we should resist them with a declaration of the full truth. These fiery darts can be quickly extinguished by the shield of faith.

> Take up the shield of faith, with which you can extinguish
> all the flaming arrows of the evil one (Eph 6:16).

When the evil one puts dangerous thoughts into our minds, they should be countered with words of faith. Simply thinking about a relevant promise of God's will extinguish the thought, rendering it harmless. Dangerous thoughts can be destroyed with a declaration of faith based on the revelation in God's word.

God does not make people sick.

Sickness is not normal for Christians.

Yahweh Rapha hates sickness.

Declarations of faith destroy the arguments and pretensions that oppose God. Anointed songs of praise and worship are another great way to declare our faith.

Jesus resisted the devil's words by quoting the scriptures; he did not argue or shout. He calmly spoke relevant scriptures claiming them for himself (Luke 4:1-12). He commanded Satan to "get behind him". This is how we can use the Shield of Faith to kill the fiery darts of the enemy.

Withdrawing Permission

The first step to getting free from existing sickness is to withdraw permission for its presence in our body. This is what the blind man did when he met Jesus.

> The blind man said, "Rabbi, I want to see" (Mark 10:51).

He had probably accepted the thought that he would be blind for life. When he heard about Jesus' ministry, he rejected that scheme. He declared that he had changed his mind by saying he wanted to see.

Christians who have been sick for a long time can begin the process by declaring that the sickness has no right to be in their body. The best way is to say,

> I want to be healed.

> This sickness does not belong in my body.

Withdrawal of permission may not be sufficient to get healing. This is a spiritual battle and our enemy is a cheat. If we withdraw permission from sickness, its legal right to remain in our bodies is gone. However, the sickness may try to remain as a squatter or trespasser. Jesus warned that an evil spirit whose lease agreement is terminated will often return with some strong companions and live in the house as a squatter. They do not respect a court order, so they can only be forced out by superior physical power.

> When it arrives, it finds the house swept clean…. Then it goes and takes seven other spirits… and they go in and live there (Luke 11:25-26).

Jesus was speaking about evil spirits, but the same principle applies to sickness. It usually tries to stay on in our lives after we have cancelled its lease. We may need to join with faithful friends to force the unwanted sickness to leave. In tough cases where the sickness has deep roots, it might be necessary to call in the elders to get victory.

Destroying Strongholds

Sometimes a stronghold of sickness may have to be demolished one layer at a time. Several deceptions may have become so entwined with a sick person's life that they will have difficulty in recognising them. They may need help from friends with words of knowledge and insights to disentangle the roots and obtain insight into their problem.

Strongholds are destroyed by the knowledge of God. If the sick person has a gap in their understanding of God's character, they may need Christian friends to teach them the truth.

> The LORD is my light and my salvation—
> whom shall I fear?
> The LORD is the stronghold of my life—
> of whom shall I be afraid (Psalm 27:1).

Love of God should be the only stronghold in our life.

6
Direct Attack

Sin and deception can give Satan access to our lives, but sometimes he just attacks directly without permission. He is a cheat and will do anything to win. Satan's objective is to steal, rob and destroy (John 10:10). Sickness is his best method for crippling Christians, because most are not aware of where the attack came from. We assume that we just got sick and do not realise that he is having a go at us.

We often gradually accept sickness without wondering where it came from. We get a headache or a sore foot and just accept it, without realising that Satan is trying us out and testing our limits. If we accept insignificant sicknesses from him, he can give us more, when he chooses. He will do this at key times when he wants to disrupt our Christian service. Sickness will usually take hold slowly, but we are gradually robbed of our ability to serve Jesus.

Our bodies are a battleground and sickness is Satan's weapon against us. The Holy Spirit is our weapon against him. Sickness is a confrontation between the powers of darkness and the power of God. Healing and deliverance manifest in the Kingdom of God (Luke 9:2).

The devil often attacks when we go "all out for God". An example from the New Testament is Epaphroditus (Phil 2:26-27). He was so ill that he almost died. This was probably an attack of the devil to disrupt his service of the Lord. Similarly, Satan attacked Eutychus, to disturb a key meeting between Paul and the elders of the church (Acts 20:9-11). Tabitha was a key leader in the church at Joppa. Satan tried to halt this work by attacking her with sickness (Acts 9:36-41).

Key 8: Resist Every Attack

The Bible urges us to resist Satan when he attacks.

> Be self-controlled and alert. Your enemy the devil prowls around like a roaring lion looking for someone to devour. Resist him, standing firm in the faith (1 Peter 5:8-9).

> Submit yourselves, then, to God.
> Resist the devil, and he will flee from you (James 4:7).

These verses also apply to sickness. When sickness intrudes in our lives without cause, we should command it to leave.

Sickness can be resisted with words of faith, when it attacks. If I feel my foot is getting sore, I do not have to accept the pain but can resist it. God has given me authority over sickness and over my body, so I can speak to sickness and command it to leave my body.

> Jesus bought my life on the cross.

> My body belongs to him.

> He has not given permission for it to be sick.

> This pain has no right to be in my body.

> My body is the temple of the Holy Spirit, so sickness does not belong in it.

> Jesus dealt with sickness on the cross.

Sickness is an intruder that has no right to be in our lives. Our immediate response should be to command it to leave.

If we do not resist sickness, we are implicitly giving it permission to be there. We are accepting the lie that sickness is normal for Christians, which is one of the fiery darts described in the previous chapter. We must resist it with words of faith. We often say no to sin. We need to say no to sickness more often.

Authority and Power

Authority and power are different and both are needed to destroy sickness. A judge has legal authority, but the police have physical power. A judge can declare that the owner of a property should have access and that a squatter must leave. However, the squatter can ignore the judge. The police have the physical power to the remove the squatter from the property according to the judge's decision.

Christians have authority over their lives, but as humans, we have very limited power. The Holy Spirit has enormous power, but no authority over our lives unless we give it to him. Christians have authority over sickness, but we have very little power. The Holy Spirit has power over sickness, but can only act, if he is given authority.

Authority and power are both needed to defeat sickness. I can withdraw the authority of a sickness to be in my body, but I do not have the physical power to force it to leave. Christians must learn to exercise their authority and release the Holy Spirit's power. We sometimes make a lot of noise as a substitute for power, but sickness is not fooled. The Holy Spirit has the physical power to force sickness to leave our bodies, but we must give him authority to use his power before he can act.

When we resist sickness by commanding it to leave, this is like a court order removing its authority to be there. Sometimes the sickness will ignore the court order. The

Holy Spirit has the police power to evict the sickness from our bodies. We must invite him to come and force it out.

Healing needs authority and power. Authority commands the sickness to leave. Power enforces the spoken command.

Willing and Able

The Holy Spirit is willing and able to deal with sickness.

- The Holy Spirit has infinite power. The powers of evil are no match for him. When they come up against him, it is no contest.
- The Holy Spirit loves to heal the sick. He is longing to evict sickness from our bodies.
- He lacks authority in our lives unless we give it to him.

The Holy Spirit is willing and has the power, but he is respectful when dealing with Christians. He will not force us to do anything. He respects our freedom, so he will not push his way in if he is not invited. He can only deal with sickness when the issue of authority is settled.

If nothing happens when we invite him to evict a sickness, it is never because he is unwilling or too weak. The only thing that could prevent him would be an authority issue that has not been sorted. If something we have said or done is still giving the sickness permission to be in our lives, he will not act against our authority. Therefore, if the sickness does not go when we give the Holy Spirit authority to remove it, we must be hanging onto thoughts or pretensions that overrule his authority. These need to be broken before he can go to work. The Holy Spirit cannot destroy these agreements for us. We have to take the permission back from sickness, because we gave it authority in the first place.

Deal with the Mess

When evil spirits leave, they do not clean up the mess they have made before they go. They leave a lot of junk behind. They do not kill their viruses and take their arthritis with them. They do not destroy the cancer cells that they have inserted. They often leave genetic damage that affects subsequent generations. We need the angels to come in and remove the junk. We need the Holy Spirit to recreate the body or restore DNA back to what God created it to be.

Angels support the Holy Spirit. He is holy and good, so he cannot touch evil. The angels do the dirty work that he cannot do. They destroy the viruses, bacteria and bad DNA that the spiritual powers of evil use to create sickness.

The Holy Spirit is creative, so he does not destroy stuff. He undertakes creative miracles. He can restore limbs and organs. In contrast, the angels destroy the junk that evil spirits leave behind when they are pushed out.

They work together. When God is healing cancer, the angels destroy the cancerous cells that the spiritual powers of evil have created, while the Holy Spirit creates new cells to replace them.

In many situations, the command "Be healed in Jesus' name" will be sufficient to complete the healing. Sometimes we will need to specifically invite the Holy Spirit and the angels to come and do a complete clean up.

Key 9: Resist Together

If we cannot resist sickness on our own, we should invite other Christians to resist with us. Sickness is tough to handle. Resisting Satan, while standing alone, is almost impossible. It is hard to have faith when burdened with sickness. Resisting is hard when we are weak or unwell. We all need others to stand with us and do battle on our behalf. This is the main reason that the modern church does not have victory over sickness. Christians are often isolated, so Satan is able to pick them off one at a time. Christians have compassion for friends who are sick, and often ask God to heal them, but they rarely go into battle against the sickness.

Paul left Trophimus sick at Miletus (2 Tim 4:20). This is the only case of sickness in the New Testament that was not healed. There is no explanation, but Paul complains that his colleagues had deserted him and left him alone. I presume that he was isolated and under pressure, so he did not have the strength to overcome the attack on Trophimus. No one was standing with him.

Victory over sickness comes from being in relationship with Christian friends, who will go into battle against an attack of sickness and push through to victory. Resisting an attack of sickness is difficult if you are standing alone. Christians need to be with people who have victory over sickness.

Two or three people have more authority than one standing on their own. The sick person might not be that confident in resisting sickness. If some friends join in declaring that the sickness has no legal right to be in his body, the sick person will be more resolute. The faith of friends can be really important.

- The paralytic had friends with faith for him to be healed (Luke 5:18-20).
- The man by the pool had no friends to stand with him (John 5:5-7).

A sick person may be so overwhelmed that they struggle to have faith and speak with authority. Friends can add their faith and authority.

Shields of Faith
We cannot use the spiritual armour in isolation. The Shield of Faith described in Ephesians is oblong like the shields used by riot police. Roman soldiers could form a line and lock their shields together in a continuous barrier. If one was attacked, the others did not watch and criticise (as often happens when a Christian gets sick), they joined together to

protect him against the attack. When they stood shoulder-to-shoulder with shields in place, they could withstand a torrent of arrows and spears.

We must learn how to stand together with Christians to resist attacks of sickness. This level of solidarity does not come automatically by being part of a church, but by being in strong relationships with other Christians, who know us enough to understand the nature of the attack and love us enough to stand with us.

The shield of faith cannot cover our backs. The spiritual armour is only effective, if we are standing together in unity with other believers.

Elders

If the attack is really tough, we should call in the big guns. This is why James urged the sick person to go their elders.

> Is any one of you sick? He should call the elders of the church to pray over him and anoint him with oil in the name of the Lord (James 5:14).

If a Christian is unable to deal with the attack with the help of friends, their elders should be able to do the job. The elders of the church should have experience in dealing with serious attacks of sickness. They will join together with the friends of the sick person to get victory.

Peter and Dorcas

Peter demonstrated the way that elders should deal with sickness when Dorcas died in Joppa. He went to Joppa as an elder, because something was wrong in the church. The devil had scored a "home run" in this infant church, so Peter went and tipped the battle back the other way.

It is not clear why there were no elders in Joppa who could deal with this problem. Possibly none had been raised up at this early stage of the gospel advance, or maybe the elders were inexperienced and just accepted that Docas's death was inevitable. Anyway, some of the disciples knew they should call on an elder to deal with the attack.

> Lydda was near Joppa; so when the disciples heard that Peter was in Lydda, they sent two men to him and urged him, "Please come at once!" (Acts 9:38).

Peter came to Joppa and took the battle to the enemy.

> Peter sent them all out of the room; then he got down on his knees and prayed. Turning toward the dead woman, he said, "Tabitha, get up." She opened her eyes, and seeing Peter she sat up (Acts 9:40).

Peter prayed and got assurance from God that her life on earth was not complete. Once he knew that this was an attempt by the devil to take out a key leader in a new church, he resisted the devil by commanding her to sit up. She was healed immediately. Peter restored the church in Joppa to the way that God wanted it to be. Sickness and death had intruded where they did not belong, so Peter whacked them out of the park.

When Paul was speaking to the church in Troas, a young man called Eutychus fell out of a window and died. Paul went down and laid on him to bring the man back to life. Paul was acting as an elder to correct something that had gone wrong in a church. The devil had killed a key young man whose role on earth was not finished. Paul restored him so that the church would be complete. If he had let the devil win, this church would have been weaker in two ways. It would have lost a valuable member, but more importantly, the faith of the church would have been crushed.

Key 10: Resist in Rest

All Christians should abide in Jesus. We must avoid a false understanding of spiritual warfare that confuses resisting, with striving. A flurry of activity and noise will not gain victory over a spiritual attack. We do not need to "babble on like the pagans" (Matt 6:7). Victory does not come from many words or noisy commands. These activities are reliant on human strength, which is sin.

> In repentance and rest is your salvation,
> in quietness and trust is your strength (Is 30:10).

We must be careful not to get into striving against the enemy, because striving makes us weak. Satan was defeated by Jesus on the cross, so all the "heavy lifting" has been done. We resist the enemy by "standing" in what Jesus has finished. We need to learn how to resist by resting in Jesus.

Resisting becomes easier, if we understand that the devil usually works by bluffing us into accepting his authority and power. We can resist his ideas by thinking or speaking the promises of God. This does not require a noisy activity. We resist sickness by declaring words of faith and inviting the Holy Spirit to remove it. The Holy Spirit does the hard work, so we do not need to strive or make a noise.

Submission and spiritual protection go together. Peter set out the pattern of submitting and resisting (1 Peter 5:5-9):

- Submit to one another
- Submit to your elders
- Submit to God
- Be vigilant
- Resist the devil
- Stand in the faith.

Submission comes before resisting and standing. The Greek word translated as "stand" is "histemi". It means stand firm, or hold one's ground. The Greek word for "resist" is "ant-histemi". It comes from the same root and means to "stand against". When Paul said that elders would watch over us (1 Tim 5:17), he used the Greek word "pro-histemi", which means "stand before". When we submit to our elders, they are standing before us and with us against evil. We must stand in submission before we can stand against evil.

Too many modern Christians are wandering around in isolation, because submission has become a dirty word in the modern world. We live an individualistic culture, where letting another person tell us what to do is seen as a sign of weakness. Submission to others is seen as immature, but our stubborn individualism comes at a huge cost, because without submission to others, we cannot stand against evil.

Submission and Spiritual Authority

When we submit to other Christians, we give them authority to act on our behalf against evil. God has made me free, so other people can only have authority in my life, if I give it to them. I give another person authority in my life by submitting to them. If I submit to friends in my church, they have authority to resist evil on my behalf. The more I submit to them, the more spiritual authority they will have to resist any evil that is attacking me.

Key 11: Resisting means Submission

This relationship between spiritual authority and submission is not well understood. We often ask other Christians to pray for us, but without much affect, because they have very little authority in our lives. They do not have authority, because we have not given it to them. We tend to assume that a large number of people praying for us will be more effective against the attacks of the enemy. This is a fallacy. When resisting evil, two or three Christians who have real authority in our lives, because we have submitted to them, will be much more effective.

The word "stand" is plural, so standing is not something that we do on our own. We must stand together with others to achieve victory. A soldier standing alone, outside authority, will be easily defeated.

Letter of James

James outlines a two-level defence against sickness.

	Sin	Deception and Attack
Friends	Therefore **confess your sins to each other.** My brothers, if one of you should wander from the truth and someone should bring him back, remember this: Whoever turns a sinner from the error of his way will save him from death and cover over a multitude of sins (James 5:16,19)	**Pray for each other** so that you **may be healed.** The prayer of a righteous man is powerful and effective. Elijah was a man just like us. He prayed earnestly that it would not rain, and it did not rain on the land for three and a half years. Again he prayed, and the heavens gave rain, and the earth produced its crops (James 5:16-18)
Elders	If he has sinned, he will be **forgiven** (James 5:15)	Is any one of you **sick?** He should **call the elders of the church to pray over him and anoint him** with oil in the name of the Lord. And the prayer offered in faith will make the sick person well; the Lord will raise him up (James 5:14-15).

At the first level, we have Christian friends. If we sin, they will challenge us. We can confess our sins to one another to get free of the sickness brought by sin. If we have accepted wrong ideas about sickness, they will help us to see the truth. If we have been attacked by sickness, our friends can pray together with us, when permission has been withdrawn, and force it to leave. Victory over sickness comes through strong relationships with other Christians.

Elders operate at the second level. If our friends cannot get victory over serious sickness, we should call on them. Elders should be able to deal with sickness, whether it comes by sin, deception or direct attack. If there is a problem with sin, the elders will have the discernment to find the underlying cause of it and get the sick person forgiven. If the sickness remains as a squatter, the elders will have the faith needed to force illegal sickness to leave. Victory over sickness comes from being submitted to elders who have the faith to heal.

The text of James 5:14-15 is interesting. It says that the elders should pray "over" him, or more literally "upon". This gives the sense that the elders will pray about the person's situation. They will do this to find the cause of the sickness, before deciding what to do.

The remedy is interesting, too. James does not tell the elders to pray in the feeble pleading way that we often pray. He actually does not use the common word for prayer. He uses the Greek word ευχη (euke), which can also be a vow. So a "prayer of faith" is not a request to God, but a strong declaration of faith. The elder's words should have a prophetic edge. Elijah is an example. He did not ask God to send a drought, but simply declared there would be no rain or dew for three years (James 5:17; 1 Kings 17:1). Earnest prayer or declaration of faith heals the sick Christian.

The word for "sick person" is καμνω (kamno), which comes from the word for toil, and primarily means to be tired or weakened. The verb used in the expression "the Lord will raise him up" is εγειρω (egeiro), which means awaken from sleep, or figuratively to raise from the sleep of sickness. James describes a person who has been overcome in the struggle against the enemy's attack being stirred up and strengthened by the faith and declarations of their elders.

The message of James 5:14-16 is simple and not hard to interpret. It says that the sick person will be healed. There are no ifs, no buts and no maybes. The declaration offered in faith will make the sick person well.

Key 12: Faith is Essential

Faith is the key to claiming our inheritance. The scriptures teach that we receive everything earned by Jesus through faith. If we remember that salvation and healing are the same word, Eph 2:8 can be translated as,

> By grace you have been *healed*, through faith (Eph 2:8).

Without faith, we cannot receive the healing that God has promised (Heb 11:6).

Faith is not a desire to be healed. Nor is faith a belief in the truth of Christian healing. We can believe that Jesus' wounds earned healing for Christians, but not have faith to receive healing. Demons believe that God exists, but they do not have faith to receive salvation. Faith is a certainty deep in our being that God will do what he has promised.

Faith and Action

Faith has two aspects.

> If you declare with your mouth, "Jesus is Lord," and believe in your heart that God raised him from the dead, you will be saved (Romans 10:9).

Faith begins with belief in the heart. What is in the heart must be manifested in some word or action. The action produced by faith is a declaration that Jesus is Lord.

Faith =   {Believe in heart
           {Confess with lips.

The Greek word for confess is "homologesis". It means "same word". When confessing, we agree with God's word.

Faith is certainty in the heart, but it also requires some action to make it real. Faith without action is just a rattling gong (James 2:17-18). This can be seen in the healings described in Matthew 8 and 9. The person being healed always took some action or made a declaration that demonstrated the faith in their heart.

- The leper said to Jesus, "You can make me clean!"

- The centurion told Jesus "Do not come, but just say a word".
- The ruler said, "Put your hand on her and she will live."
- The bleeding woman touched Jesus' garment.
- The blind men said, "Yes!", when asked if he was able to heal them.

Each person made a statement or took an action that demonstrated their faith.

Faith is Evidence of the Unseen

The writer of the letter to the Hebrews says that,

> Faith is the substance of things hoped for,
> the evidence of things not seen (Heb 11:1).

Faith is not the same as hope. Hope is uncertain, whereas faith is certain. Many Christians hope that God will heal them, but that is not faith. Faith gives substance to hope. The word "substance" refers to a title deed, so faith gives us ownership of what we hope for.

Faith is evidence or proof of things that we cannot see. The Bible tells us that there are two types of "things" in this life: seen and unseen.

> We do not look at the things that are seen, but at the things which are not seen. For the things which are seen are temporary, but the things which are not seen are eternal (2 Cor 4:18).

The things that we can see are temporary. The unseen things come from God and are eternal. Faith is being certain of things that are not seen. God may have promised them to us, but we need faith because we cannot see them yet. When we receive them, we no longer need faith, because we can see them. Faith is only required for things that are unseen.

Living by Faith

Paul told us how Christians should live.

> We live by faith, not by sight (2 Cor 5:7).

We should not live according to the things that we cannot see. We live by faith, which is certain about the things we cannot see. God has promised that we are healed by Jesus' wounds. This is an eternal promise of something we do not yet see. We cannot see Jesus' wounds, or the healing they have earned. We cannot see the demons and sickness fleeing. Faith is being certain of these things and living as if they have happened.

If I have money in my bank account, I cannot see a heap of notes and coins with my name attached to them. I will have a bank statement that is evidence of what I have in my account. My wallet may be empty, but I can go into a shop and buy something using my bankcard with full confidence that I can pay for it. I have faith to make purchases, based on the evidence of my statement. I do not act on my empty wallet that I can see, but on the basis of the money in my bank account that I cannot see. I will only run into problems if the bank does not keep its promises, or if I spend more than is in my account.

Christians know that God will keep his promises. His word states that Jesus has earned healing for us. If Jesus has put healing "in the bank" for us, we can start living as if we have it. In this context, faith is acting as if I have received the healing that Jesus earned for me. My symptoms may say that I am sick, but the Word of God says that I am healed. This is the conflict between what is seen and what is unseen. Faith is certain of what is unseen.

If I continue to walk everywhere, after someone has bought me a car, most people would say that I am a fool. This suggests that there is something wrong with the church continuing to be full of sickness, when we have a bank statement declaring that Jesus has purchased healing for us. We need faith to appropriate the health that Jesus has put onto our statements.

On the other hand, faith is not presumption. Belief in the heart must come first. If we have faith, action will follow; but action will not produce faith. Confessing or acting without faith is presumption. Faith is a gift from God. We must receive faith from him before we can do anything.

Symptoms

Abraham showed the correct way to deal with symptoms.

> Without weakening in his faith, he faced the fact that his body was as good as dead--since he was about a hundred years old--and that Sarah's womb was also dead. Yet he did not waver through unbelief regarding the promise of God, but was strengthened in his faith (Rom 4:19-20).

Abraham faced his symptoms squarely. He did not pretend they were not there. He faced the facts, but did not waver through unbelief. His faith was not weakened, but was strengthened by the promise of God. Despite the symptoms declaring his age, he kept on preparing for the birth of a son.

The problem for modern people is that we can see the "things that are seen" very clearly. We have scans and X-rays that help us to see tumours and fractures much better than was possible in the past. We have tremendous evidence of the things that are seen and tend to focus on them. We have become accustomed to living in what we see.

Sickness among Christians is not proof that God does not heal. God dealt with our sin on the cross. The fact that we still sin does not imply that God does not save us from sin. It just shows that we are a bit slow to take up the salvation that Jesus had earned for us. The problem is with us, not with the cross. In the same way, the fact that we get sick does not mean that God does not heal. The problem is with us (or our church). We should never let our experience determine our theology. Our theology and our beliefs about healing must be based on what God has said and done.

Increasing Faith

The first step is for the church to be honest about its lack of faith. We should not pretend, or go into condemnation, but should look to God for a solution.

1. We can pray for faith (Mark 9:21-24). The Holy Spirit will increase our faith if we ask for it.

2. We should immerse ourselves in the biblical accounts of Jesus' healing. Faith comes from hearing the word (Rom 10:17). As we feed on the promises of God, our faith will grow.

3. We should seek to be filled with the Spirit. Faith is a gift of the Spirit (1 Cor 12:9), so the Holy Spirit is the source of faith. Stephen and Barnabas were men who were full of the Spirit and faith (Acts 6:5,8; 11:24). People who are full of the Spirit will also be full of faith.

4. We should start on easy things. As we rejoice in small victories, our faith will increase. Seeing miracles increases faith (John 2:23).

5. We should get with other Christians to pray. Christians should work in a group.

    - There is power in agreement. Jesus promised that when two or three people work together, he would be with them (Matt 18:19-20, Acts 3:4).
    - Our faith will be stronger when we operate with other Christians we trust. Peter and John had faith to heal the lame man, because they were proclaiming the gospel together in unity (Acts 3:4).
    - Working in a group releases the gifts of the Spirit.

Faith overcomes fear. This is important, because fear of sickness is something that we have to deal with. The word cancer really strikes fear in people's hearts. The trouble is that fear kills faith (Luke 8:50). As faith grows, fear will be squeezed out.

7

Practical Issues

Pray in Private

Understanding the cause of sickness will dramatically change the way that the elders minister to Christians. The process will be much slower, but more thorough. Ministry to sick Christians should generally take place in private, often in someone's living room. The sick person will ask some friends or the elders to come and pray (James 5:14). A lot of personal stuff may need to be dealt with, and this is best done in private. The sick person should not be prayed for at the front of the church, in view of the entire congregation. Doing this is a distortion of the other healing stream. Publicity is fine, when using the healing gifts for evangelism, but praying about the cause of sickness should be done away from the public gaze.

Peter demonstrates this contrast. He healed a paralytic in Joppa in public.

> There he found a man named Aeneas, a paralytic who had been bedridden for eight years. "Aeneas," Peter said to him, "Jesus Christ heals you. Get up and take care of your mat." Immediately Aeneas got up. All those who lived in Lydda and Sharon saw him and turned to the Lord (Acts 9:33-35).

Peter was operating as an evangelist, so the healing was public and many came to the Lord. When he got to Joppa, he operated differently, because Dorcas was a Christian. Peter went into her room and prayed on his own. He did not know the cause of her illness, so he sought the wisdom of the Lord in privacy. The cause might be something that would embarrass her friends and family if it were revealed in public. The Lord might have told Peter not to worry, because he wanted Dorcas to be with him, but I suspect that he already knew that was not the case when he decided to go to Joppa. Peter found out what was going on in private.

Work in Teams
Several people should pray about the sick person. James talks about elders (plural). There might be a team of elders and a couple of friends present. Working with a healing team will ensure that all the spiritual gifts needed are present. We should not expect one person to have all the gifts.

Four spiritual gifts might be needed to get a sick Christian healed: word of knowledge, discernment, faith, healing. The gifts of discernment and word of knowledge will often be more important than the gift of healing. The latter gift is more important for evangelism, but discernment will be more important in a healing team dealing with Christians.

The Holy Spirit can give all these gifts to one person, but he prefers to give them to different people so they will work together. He does this to strengthen the body.

If someone gets a word of knowledge about a sickness, we should not assume that they have the faith to heal the sick person. The Spirit may have given the gift of faith to someone else in the body. For example, when the man at the Beautiful Gate was healed, Peter did the talking, but he said, "Look at **us**!" (Acts 3:4). John may have had the gift of faith that produced the healing.

Get the Reason

The first step is to find out why the enemy has been able to inflict the sickness. This is important. Everything is "trial and error" until the cause has been identified. The healing team should wait on God (for days if necessary) until they know whether the sickness is the result of sin or deception or direct attack. The gift of discernment and word of knowledge will be important for answering this question. Again, this is very different from the modern ministry of healing, where the first step is to pray for the person to be healed. Praying is risky, if the reason for the sickness is not known. This is one reason why many Christians are not healed. Once the cause is understood, the team can deal with it.

1. Sin

If the healing team discerns that the cause is sin, they should be compassionate when conveying this to the sick person. They may need guidance from the Holy Spirit about how to communicate a hard message. Nathan spoke to David in a parable, when he wanted him to understand that he had sinned (2 Sam 12:1-7).

The sick person may need time to work through the issue. The solution to sin is repentance, but only the Holy Spirit can produce repentance (John 16:8). The healing team will give the Holy Spirit time (often several days) to do this work. Praying for healing before repentance is complete might lead to lack of victory. Once the person has repented, they may need to confess the sin to their friends or to the elders. Those who confess their sins will be healed (James 5:16).

Once the person repents, the symptoms of the disease should disappear, but sometimes prayer by friends or elders may be needed to shift them. The healing team should declare that the sickness no longer has any authority to remain with the person and command it to leave. They will release the Holy Spirit to restore the parts of the body that are damaged. Faith will be important.

> The prayer of faith will make the sick person well (James 5:15).

2. Deception and Control

If the sickness is the result of deception and control, the process will be different. The emphasis will be on exposing the thoughts and beliefs that give the sickness authority to attack the Christian. A word of knowledge or gift of discernment might be needed to identify spiritual strong-holds or controlling deception.

Once the root of the problem has been exposed, the healing team will agree with the sick person on withdrawing any permission that has been given to the sickness. They will unite in inviting the Holy Spirit to force the sickness out. They will counter the deception, by giving him permission to do his work.

3. Direct Attack

If the sickness is a direct attack from the enemy, the healing team should resist the sickness directly. They should not plead with God to heal the sick person, but will resist the sickness by commanding it to leave.

Persistence

Getting complete victory may take some time. This is the nature of spiritual warfare. Sometimes an initial attack may fail and the army may have to retreat and regroup before attacking again. Even when the army has a quick initial victory, the battle is not won. The enemy may counterattack again and again over several months, before giving up.

Satan does not stop trying, just because he gets one hiding. He always comes back for more. The healing team must be ready for these counter attacks. One of the healing team should keep in regular contact with the person healed. They will help them avoid thoughts or words that would give the sickness permission to return. They will pray for their faith to be strengthened.

If the sickness returns, the team will come together to deal with it. They will not blame the sick person for lack of faith, but will see it as a problem that they must deal with together. The team will stay on the case, until Satan gives up and goes off somewhere else. This is a battle of wills, but if the Christians understand their authority, they will always win.

Walk in Health
The person healed will have to learn to walk in the truth. John prayed that believers would live in health.

> Dear friend, I pray that you may enjoy good health and that all may go well with you, even as your soul is getting along well. It gave me great joy to have some brothers come and tell about your faithfulness to the truth and how you continue to walk in the truth. I have no greater joy than to hear that my children are walking in the truth (3 John 3-5).

We must learn to live in the truth that Jesus has destroyed sickness.

Deal with Failure
Those praying with sick Christians must always deal with the consequences of their actions. We are human, so things will often not work out as we expect. If a situation goes wrong, we must find out why and deal with it. We must never dump the responsibility for our failure on the sick person. Elders have a particular responsibility in dealing with any failures. If the sick person is left unhealed, they will feel that they do not have enough faith, or that God does not love them. They could end up feeling condemned and vulnerable.

Sickness can be hard to handle, so we must not pretend it is easy. If Christians cannot get victory over sickness, the elders of their church should accept responsibility. They should be willing to admit that they do not have enough wisdom or faith. Christian elders and pastors must stop dumping their lack of faith on people who are sick. Many of the people in their churches long to be healed. They have prayed and tried to believe. They should not be condemned. The failure rests with a church that has lost its inheritance.

The time has come for this burden to be lifted off the sick and put back where it belongs, on the elders of the church. Once Christian elders take responsibility for their lack of faith and failure to defeat sickness, they can seek out God's solution. Once they get his answer, they can start battling through to victory to receive all that Jesus promised.

Avoid Perversity
Lack of faith is a serious problem for the modern church and the reason we receive so little. Jesus called his followers an unbelieving generation (Matt 17:17). In many ways, the same description applies to the modern church. We have been made into an unbelieving generation by our education and scientific approach to life. We have forgotten that true science cannot deal with the spiritual dimension of life.

Our perverse lack of faith trusts many odd things:
- Copper bracelets,
- Bee venom,
- Magnetic blankets
- Steel needles.

Christians talk of their favourite cure, but we seldom hear them declaring what God can do. Some of the things they trust do work for a time. Satan is quite happy to take away the symptoms for a while, to get us to believe in a lie. However, in the end, the only way to deal with a satanic attack is to stand against him holding the shield of faith. Like the man beside the pool, Christians are looking to other things, when they should be looking to Jesus (John 5:7).

Spiritual Covering

Spiritual protection is not taken seriously by the modern church. However, spiritual warfare is not something that we are free to do when we choose, because we are engaged in it all the time. We are on the winning side because Jesus has won the victory, but we must never be complacent.

Part of the problem is that many Christians have been deceived by a false doctrine of "covering". This doctrine states that we are covered and protected from evil by submitting to a pastor-leader or being part of a church. However, there are several problems with this doctrine.

- The doctrine of covering is not taught in the scriptures, but is based on an allegorical interpretation of Boaz's garment in the book of Ruth and the cloud in Exodus. The robe and the cloud are symbolic and not the cause of protection. Trusting in a vague, ambiguous doctrine of spiritual protection is dangerous.

- The covering doctrine makes spiritual protection into something magical. Belonging to a church does not automatically guarantee that a person is protected from attack. In reality, protection comes from being in relationship with Christians who recognise an attack and will battle through to victory. Ruth was protected because Boaz was a man of authority and she submitted to him. The Israelites were protected by the presence of God under the spiritual authority of Moses.

- A pastor can only provide protection that is as good as his own. Many Christians do not realise that the pastors they trust are extremely vulnerable to spiritual attack, so they cannot provide strong protection for others. People who submit to pastors and elders who do not have victory over sickness are vulnerable to attacks by the same sickness. They need spiritual protection that works.

Christians everywhere are being decimated by evil because they do not understand the real nature of spiritual protection.

Key 13: Live in the Right Place

Territory and geography are vital for spiritual warfare. The spiritual pressure in a city or country is not evenly distributed, so the place where we choose to live or work may affect our health.

- If we live close to the stronghold of the spiritual forces that dominate our city, we may experience stronger attacks of sickness. Christians are often heroic and choose to live in the toughest part of the city. However, a wise general attacks where the enemy is most vulnerable, not where it is the strongest.

- If the intensity of the Holy Spirit's presence is strong in the area where we live, because there are more Christians there, walking in health will be easier.

- When a Christian lives in isolation from other Christians, they are vulnerable to attacks of sickness.

- If we work at a business, where the people in authority are defeated by sickness, we may experience stronger attacks of sickness. By submitting to their authority, we open ourselves to the same attack. We should be aware of this and stand against their sickness.

- Some Christians have been attacked by sickness, when they moved from a place of spiritual safety to a house in a "better area" under more spiritual pressure. The quality of the housing will be a poor indicator of the spiritual pressure as it is discerned spiritually.

Christians should be aware of the spiritual implications when they change their place of residence. We may be called to move to an area that is spiritually tougher, but we should be prepared. If we are defeated by sickness, changing locality could be the key to getting victory over sickness.

Accusations

The book of Job explains that his sickness was caused by the spiritual powers of evil. He got sick, because Satan was able to accuse him. He is a prosecutor who attacks God's people by making accusations against them.

Satan accused Job of serving God with impure motives. He said Job was serving God for what he could get out of it. He claimed Job's love of God was really selfishness.

By making this accusation, Satan gained the right to take away Job's wealth and health. He supported his accusation with testimonies from people who knew Job well.

Job's friends came to comfort him, but when he refused to admit that he deserved his pain, they got frustrated and revealed their true thoughts about him. They accused him of greed and deceit (Job 15:5; 18:7-9; 20:19-20; 22:6-9).

People do not change their opinions about others. If Job's friends believed he was greedy and deceitful after he had suffered, they would have believed it while he was prosperous. They might not have accused Job to his face, but they would have spoken their accusations to each other, while gossiping about him.

When Satan appeared before God, he said that Job was deceitful and greedy. This is exactly what Job's friends said when he was still prosperous. The testimonies of Job's friends carried weight because they knew him well. Satan was able to make his accusation to God, because he had three reliable witnesses.

A principle of God's justice is that facts are established by the testimony of three witnesses (Deut 19:15). Satan did not make up his accusation. He just repeated the words of Job's friends. Because they were friends of Job, God had to accept their testimony. Their testimony proved Satan's case against Job, so he was legally entitled to inflict sickness on him.

God's people should understand the role of the accuser. He is looking for witnesses with a testimony he can use. When we criticise other people, Satan can pick up these testimonies and accuse them before God. If he can find three people saying the same thing, he has the right to afflict the accused person with sickness.

Many Christians are sick, because brothers and sisters in the Lord have spoken words of accusation against them and Satan has taken these words and used them as testimony to accuse them. Before they can be healed, the power of these testimonies must be broken.

Jesus warned his followers about the dangers of "careless words" (Matt 12:36). Some careless words become testimonies that Satan can use to accuse other Christians. He likes testimonies from Christians because they have more credibility. He can say, "This witness is a Christian, so their words must be reliable."

Breaking Accusations

If someone is not healed, it might be because the accuser is using accusations against them. The power of the accusations will have to be broken, before the person can be healed. The method depends on the nature of the accusation.

1. Some accusations will be true. That does not matter because Jesus dealt with all our sin on the cross. If an accusation is true, the person accused can agree, but declare the fault was already dealt with by the blood of Jesus. Acknowledging the truth of an accusation and covering it with Jesus' blood is sufficient to break its power.

2. Some accusations will be untrue. We can break their power by refusing to accept them and proclaiming God's truth instead. For example, we can declare that

we are pure and blameless, because we are washed in the blood of Jesus.

3. If the accusation takes the form of a negative prophecy, we can crush its power by declaring God's truth. Promises and prophecies that God has specifically given to the person are the best antidote.

Job appealed to God. The Father's testimony about him overturned the testimony of his friends and Job's health was restored.

Anyone struggling to be healed should ask the Holy Spirit to reveal any accusations that are holding back their healing.

False Testimony
Under the biblical model of justice, the person who gives false testimony against another can be given the penalty that their testimony would have inflicted on the victim of their lies (Deut 19:16-19). When God restored Job, his friends could have experienced what they had allowed the accuser to inflict on him. Fortunately, God asked Job to pray for them (Job 42:7-8). God heard Job's prayer and protected them from the consequences of their false testimony.

Some Christians will be sick, because they have given false testimony against a brother and sister, and they are receiving what the person they were accusing would have received, if their testimony had been accepted. A false accusation can harm a brother or sister, but it can also fall back on us, if our testimony is confirmed as false.

If the Holy Spirit convicts us of speaking words that have harmed a brother or sister, we should ask the Lord for forgiveness. We should declare to the spiritual powers of evil that we are withdrawing our testimony and that we will not testify against the person they are trying to harm.

8

Elders and Pastors

When Christians ask why God allowed someone to die, a very different question is being asked in heaven.

Why did the church allow that person to die?

Jesus has earned healing for his body, so he expects the church to put this victory to work. The main responsibility for dealing with sickness rests with elders and pastors.

> Is any one of you sick? He should call the elders of the church (James 5:14).

This is a challenging word for elders and pastors of churches with sickness. God has said to them:

> Heal the sick, raise the dead, cleanse those who have leprosy (Matt 10:8).

> Your prayer offered in faith will make the sick person well (James 5:15).

God has given elders and pastors responsibility for healing their people.

Key 14: Elders and Pastors are Responsible for Dealing with Sickness

Elders should not be appointed until they have proved they can resist sickness in their family and household. One qualification required of an elder is that they can "care for the church" (1 Tim 3:5). The Greek word translated as "care" is only used in one other place in the New Testament. The Good Samaritan used this same word when he asked the innkeeper to "care" for the wounded man until he was well (Luke 10:34-35). Potential elders should have cared for sickness in their family.

Warning to Pastors

Ezekiel had a severe warning for pastors who do not heal sickness in their flock.

> Woe to the shepherds of Israel who only take care of themselves! Should not shepherds take care of the flock...? You have not strengthened the weak or healed the sick or bound up the injured (Ezek 34:2-5).

He says that God is angry with the pastors who do not heal the sick in their flock. They should be helping those who are being attacked by the enemy and setting them free. In God's eyes, healing the sick is more important than preaching sermons. This is a serious challenge for elders and pastors.

When Jesus saw the people suffering from sickness and disease, he was filled with compassion.

> Jesus went through all the towns and villages... healing every disease and sickness. When he saw the crowds, he had compassion on them, because they were harassed and helpless, like sheep without a shepherd (Matt 9:35-36).

How did Jesus know the people were harassed by Satan and like sheep without a shepherd (pastor)? They were wasted by sickness and disease. He did not ask God to heal them, but prayed that God would provide good shepherds for them. Many Christians are still harassed and without a shepherd. The church desperately needs pastors and elders who can set their people free from sickness.

Teaching people to be satisfied with sickness is not the solution, because it devalues the work of Jesus. The disappointment will only disappear when the church is walking in all that God has promised and established through Jesus' death and resurrection. Healing is the only antidote to this disappointment.

Christians should expect their elders and pastors to heal their diseases. If they are sick, the problem is with their leaders, not with God, so crying out to him will be a waste of energy. Sick Christians can pray that God will stir up their elders and give them insight and wisdom. They can pray that their elders will grow in faith and the power of the Spirit, but pleading with God for their healing makes no sense, because he expects pastors and elders to do the job.

Questions for Pastors
When a mature Christian dies of serious sickness, their pastor often wonders why God allowed it. Few will hear God saying what Ezekiel heard,

> You have not healed the sick or bound up the injured.

We should stop saying,

> Why did God allow this to happen?

Some better questions are:

> Why did our elders allow this sick person to die?

> Why were our elders unable to heal the sick person?

> Are we praying enough for our elders and pastors?

God appoints and anoints elders with power to heal the sick. He does not mind if they admit that their faith is too weak, but they should be careful not to blame him for their failure.

When pastors and elders allow their people to get offended at God over sickness, they are letting them blame God for something, which they should be doing. Allowing people to blame God so they can wiggle out of their responsibilities is a dangerous game.

Prophets

Prophets also have responsibility, as they are experts on the truth. They should be exposing the lies of the enemy. The main reason Satan has been so successful in spreading his lies is that the prophets have been asleep. God's prophets should be destroying his deceptions.

Many Christian prophets have adopted the Old Testament prophets as their heroes, but they have not realised that their heroes all healed the sick. They heard God's voice clearly, so they knew sickness came from the devil. That is why they fought against it.

The prophetic ministry was given to build up the body of Christ. An important aspect of the prophetic task is exposing the lies that weaken the body. The church needs prophets and pastors working together for victory over sickness.

Prophetic Declarations

Prophetic declarations can be really important weapons against sickness and disease. Prophets should be declaring God's word against sickness.

> He sent forth his word and healed them (Ps 107:20).

We need more prophetic words against the schemes of the enemy:

> Bill will not die, but live to the glory of God.

> This man will complete the work he was called to do.

Jesus prophesied to a blind man:

> Go, your faith has healed you (Mark 10:52).

The church needs prophets to speak the truth about healing.

9

The Rock of Offence

Several years ago, a friend with prophetic insight challenged me to speak to the rock of offence. I did not have a clue what this meant, despite searching the scriptures over several years. However, it all became clear when I heard a message by Bill Johnson about John the Baptist. I began to understand the problem of disappointment and offence.

Many Christians have sought healing for a long time without success. In some churches, these disappointed people have been prayed for over and over again, but nothing has happened. Most have a deep sense of disappointment and have given up all hope of being healed. Some have been hurt by accusations of lack of faith. This enormous backlog of hurt and disappointment with God has never been sorted.

Key 15: Deal with Disappointment and Offence

When disappointment is frequent and unresolved, the disappointed people get offended at God. Offence produces unbelief, which shuts out the power of the Spirit. I now believe that offence at God is a major obstacle to the release of healing in the church.

Big Question

As Christians have prayed earnestly for people that they love to be healed of sickness without success, their hope has gradually subsided into despair. Because they have not been taught about the danger of being offended at God, they have often asked the big question.

Why did God allow this to happen?

This question is dangerous, because it puts God on trial. It assumes that he is responsible for what happened. If the grief is deep, the question can easily be tinged by accusation and blame. If the big question is not quickly turned around, the questioner will be offended at God. A more dangerous question soon follows.

Can I trust God?

The motivation behind this question is offence at God. It kills faith and shuts up the Holy Spirit's power. It often turns into a statement.

God does not heal everyone.

This is serious, because God cannot work in the midst of people who doubt his power or willingness to heal.

Be Honest Always

We can be totally honest with God about what is happening to us. We can say,

This pain is tearing me apart.

My heart is so heavy that I feel it will break.

I know how I should be responding, but I just cannot do it.

We do not need to pretend. We can tell the Father about our feelings and our struggles. He can cope with our honesty; but we must not tell God what he should be feeling or doing. Job is a good example. He let it all hang out, but he refused to accuse God.

> In all this, Job did not sin by charging God with
> wrongdoing (Job 1:22).

When dealing with pain and death, we can be honest with God about what is happening to us. He is glad when we are open with him and ask for help, but we must guard our hearts lest our pain turns into disappointment or offence with him. We must never question his power or his love.

Good Questions

We must learn to ask the right questions. If a Christian dies, we tend to ask accusing questions.

Why did God not heal him?

Why did God allow him to die?

We should be asking,

Have we misunderstood the Gospel?

Have we misunderstood God's promises?

Did we get something wrong?

Why is our church so powerless?

Why do our elders not have victory over sickness?

We should ask these questions without going into condemnation. We are human, so we will often get things wrong. All that God expects is that we learn from our mistakes and grow in faith.

Parable

A man had two sons. The oldest did not want to work for his Father, but wanted to start his own business in a far country. His Father gave him a million dollars to get started and off he went. The son never started the business, but frittered the money away. When it was all gone, the son contacted his Father and said that he realised that he was not cut out to be a businessman, but wanted to be a paid employee. He did not want to work for his father, because he wanted a position where he could use his creative skills.

The Father organised for a friend who owned a filmmaking business to employ his son as a creative director on a huge salary. The son only turned up to work a couple of times, so soon he was living in poverty. Some of the friends of the son started asking, "Why does his Father allow his son to live in poverty?" Those who knew the father responded, "His Father is a good and generous man. He has done more than most Fathers would do. What has the son done?"

Asking why God allowed a Christian to die is an insult to his character. God is good. He did not create sickness and there was no sickness in the Garden of Eden. Sickness was created by the devil after the fall. He invented cancer and tuberculosis. If anyone asks why God did nothing about this, the answer is that he did. God sent his son to suffer. The flesh on his back was ripped and torn by Roman whips.

> But he was pierced for our transgressions,
> he was crushed for our iniquities;
> the punishment that brought us peace was upon him,
> and by his wounds we are healed (Is 53:5).

His wounds provided healing for anyone who will believe and receive. Jesus anointed his people with the same Holy Spirit and commissioned his church to heal the sick and cleanse the leper. Given what God has done, we should be asking a different question. We should be asking why the church had not fulfilled its commission.

John's Disappointment

When John the Baptist was in prison, he sent messengers to Jesus asking if he was the messiah (Mat 11:2-3). John had seen the Holy Spirit come down and heard God speak when Jesus was baptised, so he knew who Jesus was.

> Then John gave this testimony: "I saw the Spirit come down from heaven as a dove and remain on him....I have seen and I testify that this is the Son of God" (John 1:32-34).

John had given this amazing testimony, but now he was asking if Jesus really was the messiah. The reason for his doubt was disappointment.

Jesus had promised at the beginning of his ministry that he would "proclaim freedom for the prisoners" (Luke 4:18), so John had expected to be released, but now he was stuck in prison and would likely die. No wonder he was disappointed; but he had fallen into the trap of judging Jesus by his own experience. Jesus' response to John is interesting.

> Go and tell John the things which you hear and see: The blind see and the lame walk; the lepers are cleansed and the deaf hear; the dead are raised up and the poor have the gospel preached to them. And blessed is he who is not offended because of me (Mat 11:4-6).

Jesus gave John a solution to his disappointment. He told him to look at what he was doing. We get disappointed when we focus on what we think God is not doing. The best way to deal with disappointment is to look at what God is doing. This should dispel every disappointment.

Jesus also gave a warning: "Blessed is he who is not offended because of me". To be offended at someone is to have a bad attitude towards them. Jesus' message seems harsh, but John's disappointment was dangerous, because it could have given him a bad attitude to him.

John did the right thing. When he felt disappointed, he went to Jesus and sorted things out. If we are feeling disappointed in God, we must go to him and resolve our issues. This is the best way to avoid taking offence.

The Death of John the Baptist

Jesus was tempted in every way that we are. When John the Baptist was killed, Jesus could have been disappointed. He had lost a cousin and a staunch supporter. Jesus had come to die for the people, but before he could do it, John had died for him. He had good reason to be disappointed.

> John's disciples came and took his body and buried it.
> Then they went and told Jesus. When Jesus heard what
> had happened, he withdrew by boat privately to a solitary
> place. Hearing of this, the crowds followed him on foot
> from the towns. When Jesus landed and saw a large
> crowd, he had compassion on them and healed their sick
> (Matt 14:12-14).

Jesus' response to the message that John had died was to get
away to a solitary place with his Father. When the crowds
came, the power of God flowed, because he had dealt with
his pain or disappointment.

Nazareth

When Jesus came to his own village the people were amazed,
but their amazement soon changed to questions of doubt.

> "Is this not the carpenter, the Son of Mary, and brother of
> James, Joses, Judas, and Simon? And are not his sisters
> here with us?" So they were **offended** at him (Mark 6:3).

The people of Nazareth did not get carried away by what had
happened, but tried to assess Jesus. This is a sensible thing
to do when a new messiah turns up. Their problem was that
they judged Jesus by their experience of him. The boy next
door could not be the king of Israel. David had slain a lion
and killed a Philistine giant while he was still young. Jesus
had nothing to show in Nazareth, but a few cupboards and
benches. He could not be the Messiah.

Their statements about Jesus were true. He was a
carpenter and a brother of James and the others. However,
these true statements were limited to their experience, so
they gained a distorted view of him. They did not ask what
had happened in other towns. They gave greater weight to
their own experience than to all that Jesus had done.

Their mistake was testing Jesus against their expectations
of the Messiah. Their expectations were wrong, so they were
disappointed. Their disappointment led to their being

offended by him. Offence produced unbelief, which shut down the power of God.

> Now He could do no mighty work there, except that He laid His hands on a few sick people and healed them. And He marvelled because of their **unbelief** (Mark 6:5-6).

The people of Nazareth just asked some questions about Jesus, but the scriptures say they were offended by him. Their experience illustrates a dangerous downward spiral that can affect Christians:

- Amazement
- Judging God's work against our expectations
- Disappointment
- Offence
- Unbelief
- Holy Spirit quenched
- No miracles

Offence at God produces unbelief, which limits the Holy Spirit's power.

Capernaum

The people of Capernaum demonstrate the correct way to respond. When Jesus came, they were amazed too. They asked some questions, but theirs were questions of faith, not questions of doubt.

> Then they were all amazed, so that they questioned among themselves, saying, "What is this? What new doctrine is this? For with authority He commands even the unclean spirits, and they obey Him." And immediately His fame spread throughout all the region around Galilee…. At evening, when the sun had set, they brought to Him all who were sick and those who were demon-possessed. And the whole city was gathered together at the door. Then He healed many who were sick with various diseases, and cast out many demons; and He did not allow the demons to speak, because they knew Him (Mark 1:27-28,33-34).

The pattern here is very different:

- Amazement
- Questions of faith
- Focus on what God is doing
- Acceptance
- Faith
- Healing and deliverance.

There was no offence at Jesus in Capernaum, so the power of healing flowed.

Lessons for Christians

This contrast between Nazareth and Capernaum is huge.

1. Many churches and Christians have prayed earnestly for sick people, but they have died. This has produced huge disappointment. When disappointment is frequent and unresolved, people get offended at God. This offence produces unbelief and quenches the power of the Spirit.

2. Many Christians have received prayer for healing with nothing happening. They have a deep sense of disappointment and have lost all hope. Some have been hurt by accusations of lack of faith. This huge backlog of hurt and disappointment with God has never been acknowledged.

3. One of the greatest obstacles to healing in the church is unbelief that comes through offence at God for not healing people we expected to be healed. We have allowed our disappointment to justify our offence.

4. Offence is a silent insidious sin that is mostly buried and hidden. When we are offended by someone, we often say nothing. The other person may not even know that we are offended. However, the offence still infects our relationship by eating away in our hearts and tainting everything we say and do.

5. Most Christians who are offended at God over sickness have never said what they feel out loud. They just have this feeling of being let down by God. This wrong attitude is often buried so deep in their hearts that we do not know it is there. However, it taints their thoughts and words and spoils their relationship with God. Buried offence makes faith difficult.

6. Christians can get offended over many issues. Sickness and lack of healing is the main cause of offence against God in churches that have been touched by the move of the Holy Spirit. The charismatic renewal created great expectations for healing that has never been fulfilled. Many who are disappointed have taken offence at God.

7. Turning a statement about the facts of a situation, into a statement about the nature and the character of God is dangerous. Sometimes when a respected Christian dies of an illness, Christians deal with it by saying, "God does not heal everyone". That is true as a statement of fact, because this Christian was not healed. However, "God does not heal everyone" is dangerous when it becomes a theological statement, because it suggests that God is capricious or fickle. The question oozes offence at God. Christians do not say it out loud, but they are questioning the extent of his love, his goodness or his power. The following unspoken questions make this clear.

> Why would a good God allow this to happen?

> Why could a powerful God not prevent this from happening?

> Why would a loving God allow someone to suffer in this way?

When we are offended by God, we tend to blame him for things that are evil.

8. When things go wrong, it is good to ask God why. That was John the Baptist's response. Likewise, the disciples asked Jesus why they were unable to heal the boy with the evil spirit (Mark (9:28). However, although it is good to ask why, we must be very careful about how we frame our questions. John's question was dangerous, because it judged Jesus' character and ministry on the basis of John's experience. "Are you the one" (Matt 11:3)?

   The disciples' question was better, because it tested their experience, against the standards of Jesus, "Why couldn't we…?" Their question expressed humility, not offence at God. We should be careful to ask these questions without going into condemnation. We are human, so we will often get things wrong. All that God expects is that we learn from our mistakes and grow in faith.

9. We must never ask our questions in a way that puts God on trial. We can confess our lack of faith, but we must never cast doubt on his love, or his goodness or his power. We must never ask a question that blames God. Our questions are often similar to those of the people of Nazareth. When our worship is a bit flat, we say,

   > Was the Holy Spirit here?

   The Holy Spirit is always there, so we should really be asking.

   > Have we grieved the Spirit?

   We should always ask our questions in a way that honours the Holy Spirit. Here are some humble questions that will enable us to learn.

   > Why is my grief so painful? (Because you loved them of course.)

   > Why was the church not able to heal the sick person?

What is the reason for our lack of faith?

Was there a root cause for this sickness that we missed?

Why is our church powerless against sickness?

Why are our elders unable to get victory over sickness?

The following questions are dangerous because they reflect disappointment and could lead to offence at God.

Why did God allow this to happen?

Why did God not answer our prayers?

He was a good man. Why did God not heal him?

Why has God left this lovely family without a father?

The Bible defines any question that blames or accuses God as offence at him. He wants us to talk to him about things that happen so we can learn, but we must never ask questions that put him on trial. God is love. God is good. Love and goodness are at the heart of his character. Questioning his love, or his goodness, or his power is an insult to his name. We must never shift the blame for our weakness to God.

10. Disappointment can also lead to apathy, especially for those who are young. While disappointment causes some people to get stirred up and offended at God, others slip into apathy. They respond by saying,

I don't care. I never expected anything to happen anyway.

Apathy also kills faith, because apathetic people just give up expecting anything from God. In some ways, this is worse. God can cope, if we are upset with him, but there is not much that he can do for those who do not care, because apathy quenches the Holy Spirit.

.

10
Challenge

Wires Crossed

Many Christians have been praying earnestly for healing but their prayers have not been answered. Many pastors have been praying for people who go forward at their meetings to be healed, without getting victory. The problem is that we have our spiritual wires crossed. The biblical pattern is clear.

Non-Christian	Christian
Healing is based on grace	Healing is part of the covenant
Needs a gift of healing	Needs a spiritual victory
Healing is a gift from God	Appropriating what God has already given.

Most Christians are using the wrong method when they deal with sickness. We are trying to use the gifts of healing for Christians, when we should be using them in the world for evangelism. Christians are asking God to heal them, when he has already done everything that is necessary for salvation (healing). Christians should not be asking God to heal them. They do not need to plead with Jesus for healing. He has already provided healing for us by being whipped and beaten.

We do not have to ask Jesus for his healing, but we do need to appropriate what he has already given to us. We receive what is ours by faith.

God has given his people authority over sickness, and Satan (Matt 10:1):

- Christians have authority over sickness in their bodies;
- Fathers have authority over sickness in their family;
- Elders have authority against sickness in their disciples;
- If we resist the devil together, he will flee.
- Christians preaching the gospel have authority to heal unbelievers.

Instead of asking God to heal us, we must use our authority to get rid of sickness.

When Jesus was flogged, his skin was torn open and his muscles were lacerated by several pieces of glass or bone on the end of the whip straps. Only death was necessary for forgiveness of our sins. Jesus' body was broken for our healing. If we do not walk in it, his pain is wasted.

Holy Spirit is Willing

This book outlines some important biblical principles. Of course, principles alone will not bring victory over sickness. No one has ever been healed by a principle. Healing comes through the presence of Jesus in the power of the Spirit. Faith comes from hearing the voice of God. We must learn to hear the voice of the Spirit, so that we know how they apply to the situation we are facing. As we follow the leading of the Spirit, his power will be released in our lives.

If you have read this far, you will probably be thinking,

> This all makes sense, but I find it hard believing that it is possible.

Challenge

I feel the same way, but the Holy Spirit will not let me ignore the Bible's teaching. I have seen enough healings to know what the Holy Spirit can do. I have experienced enough of his love and grace to know that he wants to do more than we can believe. Yet, I still find it hard to make this work in my life.

I challenge all Christian elders to start praying through James 5. Get together with another elder and start praying about some of the people under your care who are sick. Start seeking the wisdom of the Holy Spirit and see what he reveals. When you get a revelation, act on it. Follow his directions and you might be surprised at what he is able to do.

Many things will have to change. The role of elders will have to be transformed. A better understanding of submission and authority will have to be recovered. To achieve full spiritual protection, Christians will have to live much closer together and develop a greater level of discernment. We will have to learn what it means to stand against evil. We will have to discover what it means to love one another as Jesus loved us. We will only achieve the required level of faith by building each other up in love.

One thing should be clear from this book. We have plenty of lessons to learn and many barriers to overcome before we get complete victory over sickness. A few people standing on their own are unlikely to accomplish it. The body of Christ will need to work at this task together. As groups of elders press in to these challenges, they might achieve victory over a particular obstacle to healing. One church might get strong at dealing with curses. Another may be good at dealing with deception. Others may be better at healing evangelism. When a church gains a measure of victory, they should share their discoveries with others. In this way, the whole body will build itself up in faith.

Sickness has been one of the devil's best weapons. He will not give it up without a huge fight. Elders who try to take back the ground that we have lost will have a tremendous battle on their hands. Some will experience embarrassment and failure on the way, but the Holy Spirit can cope with that. A few will stumble and fall. We should not be discouraged by our mistakes, but should press on towards the victory promised by Jesus.

We will not get victory quickly. The current generation may not be able to do it. Shaking off the doubt that has shaped their thinking for the whole of their Christian lives might be too hard. A raft of family and national curses will have to be broken before we can get free of sickness. It might take several generations to recapture all that has been lost. The challenge will be tough, but God is looking for elders and shepherds who will press boldly into Jesus' healing and will not give up until they experience the full promise of his glorious salvation. If the church can take hold of his victory over sickness, it will be well on the way to seeing the glory of the Kingdom of God.

Fifteen Keys to Healing

About the Author

Ron McKenzie is a Christian writer
living in Christchurch, New Zealand.
During the 1980s, he served as
the pastor of a church,
but found that he did not fit that role.
He is now employed as an economist
and writes in his spare time.
He is married with three adult children.

By the Same Author

Being Church Where We Live
This challenging book offers a radical vision for the church that will stir hearts and provide guidance for people living through the Time of Distress and preparing for the glory of the Kingdom.

Times and Seasons
This book takes a different approach to God's plan for history. It begins with the ministry of Jesus and the sending of the Holy Spirit and ends with the glory of the Kingdom of God. The key seasons and the epochal events that mark the change from each season to the next are clearly described.

The Prophetic Ministry
The church urgently needs the release of the prophetic ministry. This book describes the operation of this important ministry in the church and nation.

Coming Soon

The Government of God
The Kingdom of God is one of the greatest themes of the Bible. This book will explain how the government of God can transform economic and social life.

www.ingramcontent.com/pod-product-compliance
Lightning Source LLC
Chambersburg PA
CBHW060816050426

42449CB00008B/1683